D1533914

PORTFOLIO/PENGUIN

THE WEEKEND THAT CHANGED WALL STREET

Maria Bartiromo is anchor of CNBC's *Closing Bell* (M–F, 3–5 p.m. ET), and anchor and managing editor of the nationally syndicated *Wall Street Journal Report with Maria Bartiromo*, the most watched financial news program in America.

In 1995, Bartiromo became the first journalist to report live from the floor of the New York Stock Exchange. She has covered Wall Street for more than twenty years. She joined CNBC in 1993 after five years as a producer, writer, and assignment editor with CNN Business News.

She has received numerous prestigious awards, including a 2008 News and Documentary Emmy for her coverage of the financial collapse. She received a second Emmy Award for her 2009 documentary, *Inside The Mind of Google* and was awarded a Gracie Award for a special report *Greenspan: Power, Money & the American Dream*.

In 2009, the *Financial Times* named her one of the "50 Faces That Shaped the Decade." Bartiromo was inducted into the Cable Hall of Fame Class of 2011, the first journalist to be inducted. She was named a Young Global Leader by the World Economic Forum in 2005.

She is the author of several books, including *The 10 Laws of Enduring Success* and *Use the News*.

Bartiromo writes a monthly column for *USA Today*. She has written a column for *BusinessWeek* and *Milano Finanza*, as well as *Individual Investor, Ticker,* and *Reader's Digest* magazines. She has been published in the *Financial Times, Newsweek, Town & Country, Registered Rep,* and the *New York Post*.

Bartiromo is a member of the Board of Trustees of New York University. She also serves on the board of the World Economic Forum's Young Global Leaders. She is a member of the Council on Foreign Relations, the Economic Club of New York, and the Board of Governors of the Columbus Citizens Foundation.

Bartiromo graduated from New York University, where she studied journalism and economics. She served as an adjunct professor at NYU Stern School of Business for the fall 2010 semester.

Follow Maria on Twitter@mariabartiromo
Visit www.mariabartiromo.com

The Weekend That Changed Wall Street

And How the Fallout Is Still Impacting Our World

MARIA BARTIROMO

with Catherine Whitney

PORTFOLIO / PENGUIN

PORTFOLIO / PENGUIN
Published by the Penguin Group
Penguin Group (USA) Inc., 375 Hudson Street, New York, New York 10014, U.S.A.
Penguin Group (Canada), 90 Eglinton Avenue East, Suite 700,
Toronto, Ontario, Canada M4P 2Y3 (a division of Pearson Penguin Canada Inc.)
Penguin Books Ltd, 80 Strand, London WC2R 0RL, England
Penguin Ireland, 25 St. Stephen's Green, Dublin 2, Ireland
(a division of Penguin Books Ltd)
Penguin Books Australia Ltd, 250 Camberwell Road, Camberwell,
Victoria 3124, Australia (a division of Pearson Australia Group Pty Ltd)
Penguin Books India Pvt Ltd, 11 Community Centre, Panchsheel Park,
New Delhi – 110 017, India
Penguin Group (NZ), 67 Apollo Drive, Rosedale, Auckland 0632,
New Zealand (a division of Pearson New Zealand Ltd)
Penguin Books (South Africa) (Pty) Ltd, 24 Sturdee Avenue,
Rosebank, Johannesburg 2196, South Africa

Penguin Books Ltd, Registered Offices:
80 Strand, London WC2R 0RL, England

First published in the United States of America by Portfolio Penguin, a member of Penguin
Group (USA) Inc. 2010
This paperback edition with a new epilogue published 2011

1   3   5   7   9   10   8   6   4   2

THE LIBRARY OF CONGRESS HAS CATALOGED THE HARDCOVER EDITION AS FOLLOWS:
Bartiromo, Maria.
The weekend that changed Wall Street : an eyewitness account / Maria Bartiromo,
with Catherine Whitney.
     p. cm.
Includes bibliographical references and index.
ISBN 978-1-59184-351-1 (hc.)
ISBN 978-1-59184-436-5 (pbk.)
1. Financial crises—United States—History—21st century. 2. Bank failures—United
States—History—21st century. 3. Investment banking—United States—History—21st
century. 4. Global Financial Crisis, 2008–2009. I. Whitney, Catherine. II. Title.

HB3722.B375 2010
330.973'0931—dc22   2010026892

Printed in the United States of America
Set in Minion Pro
Designed by Jaime Putorti
Title page image courtesy of istockphoto.com

Dedicated to the next generation . . .
Emerging from colleges and business schools across America,
to take your place in a system that is challenged but still great.
Learn from our mistakes, with wisdom,
creativity, humility, and integrity.

CONTENTS

CONTENTS

The Weekend
That Changed
Wall Street

Eyewitness to the Crisis

Every weekday I broadcast my show *Closing Bell* from the floor of the New York Stock Exchange. The air inside the NYSE is electric. The pace can be frantic, especially as we approach the ringing of the closing bell at 4:00 p.m. As I watch the traders hunched over their terminals and listen to the dull roar of their voices in the background, I feel a sense of awe. I am standing at the apex of the world's financial system. Everything that happens on the Big Board has consequences for billions of people, and I get to witness it all.

I realized long ago that what takes place at the NYSE is more about humans than about numbers. I know many people's eyes glaze over when they think about the financial system. It feels so abstract and unwieldy. The jargon alone is difficult to master—puts and calls, market makers, derivatives. But in the aftermath of the collapse of Wall Street that occurred in September 2008, people *did* understand that the value of their homes declined precipitously, that their retirement plans bled money, that their jobs were less secure, that their retail customers had disappeared, that business and home loans were no longer available. They saw that because of the actions of some of America's largest financial firms, their own lives were much less stable and their dreams were on hold.

With these people in mind, I decided to write *The Weekend That Changed Wall Street* in the hope that I could bring an insider's perspective to what happened to those who were directly affected. In particular, those who work outside the financial industry are still demanding explanations. They're confused by the complexity of the financial system, and they want to understand what really happened. Many people have written about the financial collapse, but I believe the position I've been fortunate to have allows me to speak as a true eyewitness, and to translate the complexities of the crisis for the average reader. In this book I will explore what happened behind closed doors and provide an intimate look at the personal stories of those involved—from the richest and most powerful to the average workers. Using my access to scores of the players (famous and not so famous), I will provide the inside story about what really happened during the weekend that changed the financial world I have covered for twenty years. I will show readers how each decision had a drastic impact on the financial system and the personal lives of those involved in it. In addition, throughout the book I will let the participants, observers, and people on the sidelines speak in their own voices—a running oral history of the crisis.

My goal here is to explain these extraordinary events in a way that ordinary people can understand—to ask and answer the questions on everybody's mind. For instance:

- How could the best and brightest in the financial services industry, with their huge compensation packages and ballyhooed brilliance, not see the meltdown coming?

How did so many of these Masters of the Universe become minions of disaster overnight?

- Is any company really too big to fail—and if so, should it be?

- Should the government spend taxpayer dollars to bail out companies whose plights are—at least in part—the result of their own mismanagement?

- Should plain vanilla banking be separated from the riskier securities business?

- Are regulators, who dropped the ball and missed the crisis in the first place, now overreaching in their efforts to "fix" the system?

- What have we learned, if anything, from the crisis? Has "business as usual" returned until the next blowup? Or has Wall Street changed?

In addressing these questions and telling the story of the biggest threat to prosperity since the Great Depression, I will invite you into my world—behind the curtain of capitalism. Knowledge is power, and my intention is to enable readers to get a better grasp of the market and a greater sense of control. It's our country, and we all have a role to play in rebuilding America's economy and making sure that our future is not jeopardized by risk-taking run wild and regulators asleep at the wheel.

Riding High Before the Fall

"It's hard to believe it can get any better."
—DAVID RUBENSTEIN, CHAIRMAN OF THE CARLYLE GROUP,
IN AN INTERVIEW WITH MARIA BARTIROMO, JANUARY 2007

DECEMBER 2006

Steve and Christine Schwarzman's annual holiday party was legendary, and normally I wasn't on the guest list. But this year was different. I ended up being invited not because of my professional relationship with Steve, chairman of the Blackstone Group, but because of my connection to his apartment, 740 Park Avenue. The previous owner, Saul Steinberg, is my father-in-law. Saul had purchased the twenty-thousand-square-foot apartment from the estate of John D. Rockefeller in 1971, for well under $300,000, and it had been his home for thirty years. My husband, Jonathan, spent much of his childhood at the Park Avenue apartment, and we held our engagement party there shortly before the sale to the Schwarzmans.

In 1999 the Steinbergs put the apartment on the market, and the Schwarzmans swept in, paying more than $30 million—the highest price ever for a Manhattan apartment at that time. Schwarzman was a Wall Street kingmaker, the man people wanted to befriend, and he was eager to demonstrate his place at the pinnacle of power and money by purchasing what was considered to be the best apartment in New York City.

Steve Schwarzman was arguably one of the most important men on Wall Street. Everyone wanted to be close to him, and in a sense everyone deferred to him because he controlled so much of the business. It was a great time to be alive and in private equity. And it was a great time to be Steve Schwarzman.

He was everywhere that year, bullish verging on boastful about the wonders of private equity and, by implication, his own golden touch. When I lunched with him at the Four Seasons restaurant in January 2006, he was ebullient. I asked him, "How easy is it to do a deal today?" and he replied provocatively, "I can do a thirty- to forty-billion-dollar deal in a very short time without debt, without covenants." He acknowledged that "in the olden days" a billion-dollar buyout was big news, but we were witnessing a phenomenal uptick in the amount of money flowing into private equity. And he added expansively, "We don't even set up a deal unless we can make at least a twenty percent annual return on investment." Our discussion in the lunchroom of power was interrupted by a steady flow of table hoppers who wanted to shake Schwarzman's hand and wish him a happy New Year—among them Sandy Weill, chairman of Citigroup; billionaire investor Ronald Perelman; and real estate kingpin Sam Zell.

Perhaps no one exemplified the stratospheric rise of private equity more than Zell. The sixty-five-year-old billionaire, the son of Jewish immigrants from Poland, was one of the wealthiest men in the world. Crusty, confident, and an unrepentant potty-mouth, Zell was both admired and feared for his ability to play extremely high stakes games. A year after I saw him at the Four Seasons, he would make the deal of the decade, selling Equity Office Properties Trust, a conglomerate of 573 properties, to Schwarzman's Blackstone Group for $39 billion. Blackstone flipped the majority of them, and Zell and Schwarzman walked away with big profits right before the real estate bust sunk most of the properties' values.

In May of 2006, I was a guest host for Charlie Rose. As I sat at Charlie's famous "table" with Schwarzman and David Rubenstein, chairman of the private-equity powerhouse Carlyle Group, I was impressed with how both men oozed confidence and optimism as they talked about making bigger and bigger deals. At one point I said, "You're in the Golden Age of private equity. Do you think the day will come when trees don't grow to the sky and the market shifts away from you?"

"Only foolish people believe that trees grow to the sky," Schwarzman said with a chuckle. "Or young people who haven't experienced trees being cut down. It's important to shine an amber light, to slow down, to not get caught up in the mania."

Indeed, Schwarzman had never been accused of getting caught up in the mania. He was a smooth operator, even-keeled—"Not a screamer," a colleague once observed. But on that day in May, he was on top of the world, and the trees in his garden did seem to be growing to the sky.

When I saw Schwarzman again in the fall, I casually asked him, "So, how's your apartment? You know, we had our engagement party there. It's an unbelievable place."

He was enthusiastic. "Maria, you've got to come over and see it." And he invited me to his holiday party.

I was interested in going, of course—not just because I was curious about the apartment, but also because I was a business reporter. Schwarzman's guest list was sure to include many of the captains of finance. So I accepted.

I hadn't realized that the Schwarzman holiday parties were always themed. That year's theme was Bond—as in *James*, not *municipal*. The host was dressed in a snazzy tux, portraying 007 with Christine shimmering at his side in a silver gown. Scantily clad "Bond girls" roamed the party serving drinks and hors d'oeuvres. There were repeated joking references to "Goldfinger" throughout the evening.

The apartment was crowded with well-known Wall Street faces. John Thain, chief executive of the NYSE, was there, having recently purchased an apartment in the building for a reported $27.5 million. I spotted a smattering of "real" celebrities, and smiled when I saw Paris Hilton holding court, surrounded by an admiring group of investment bankers from Bear Stearns, Lehman Brothers, and Goldman Sachs.

At one point in the evening I found myself in a corner chatting with Jimmy Cayne and Dick Fuld. Cayne, the flamboyant chief executive of Bear Stearns, was enjoying himself, as always, despite the buzz of criticism about his extremely large Christmas bonus of nearly $15 million. Fuld, the head of Lehman Brothers, known to be a lone wolf, hugged the corner, having private conversations and at times looking uncomfortable.

A couple of Bond girls slid over to us, and suddenly a photographer appeared. "Take your picture?" he asked. Fuld jumped up in alarm. "I'm not getting my picture taken with any Bond girls," he barked, and took off. Cayne laughed and shrugged. He didn't mind. Nothing could touch him—or so he thought.

In retrospect, the Bond theme was an interesting commentary on the era. Schwarzman might well have imagined himself as the 007 of Wall Street, smoothly sailing above the troubles that afflicted others. He appeared to enjoy playing the sophisticated man's man; the male ideal; a magnet for power, money, and women for whom danger and intrigue were all in a day's work.

Schwarzman was the envy of his peers, but he and they might have paused to consider that in 2006 the primary characteristic of James Bond was that he was an anachronism, and those who aspired to walk in his shoes were perhaps headed in the wrong direction.

This wasn't the only high-profile party the Schwarzmans threw during that season. The Bond party was followed on February 14, 2007, by a $3 million sixtieth-birthday bash for Schwarzman at the Armory in New York. Jonathan and I were in attendance there as well. The Valentine's Day birthday party got plenty of media coverage, thanks to its dazzling guest list, which included a roster of New York celebrities—Donald and Melania Trump, Barbara Walters with Vernon Jordan, Tina Brown, former New York governor George Pataki, Charlie Rose, Barry Diller, and Cardinal Egan. In addition, there was the familiar cast of Wall Street regulars—John Thain; Lloyd Blankfein, CEO of Goldman Sachs; Stan O'Neal, CEO of Merrill Lynch; Jimmy Cayne; Sandy Weill, now the former chairman of Citigroup; Jamie Dimon, CEO of JPMorgan Chase; and real estate tycoon Jerry Speyer.

Having just been to the Schwarzmans' apartment, I noticed right away that the Armory was decorated as a replica of their living room. Everything was absolute perfection, as one would expect of a party with such a hefty price tag. Schwarzman's favorite entertainer, Rod Stewart, performed. (I'm told his fee was $1 million.) Patti La-Belle sang "Happy Birthday." It was yet another lavish, over-the-top celebration of capitalism, paying homage to the new captains of finance. Life was good.

———

"It was a great age of leverage, credit, and debt entitlement," Mohamed El-Erian, CEO of Pimco, the world's largest bond investor, told me later. "People felt entitled to do all sorts of things using debt. You suddenly had a massive innovation that reduced the barriers of entry to credit markets. Wall Street believed that it could build one liquidity factory after another after another after another."

El-Erian noted that the mind-set at that point was that everything was basically stable. It was a "Goldilocks economy"—never too hot or too cold. The aura of stability led to false confidence, which led in turn to excessive leveraging and riskier activity. His take seemed to be accurate. The people whom I interviewed didn't appear to have a care in the world. But Schwarzman's opulence was starting to annoy some of his colleagues in the business. Several of them made comments to me that they wished he would stop throwing parties. Others questioned whether Schwarzman's birthday bash and his company's going public the same year represented the top for the industry.

That winter, I did a report from the World Economic Forum in Davos, Switzerland. I asked a group of very big names in finance what were the most important issues facing business. In retrospect the answers were mostly way off the mark:

- Tom Russo, vice chairman, Lehman Brothers: "Avian flu: High risk, low probability, but if it should happen, people won't come to work. We are trying to figure out how to run a firm from home."

- Martin Sullivan, CEO, AIG: "The threat of terrorism."

- Victor Chu, chairman, First Eastern Investment Group: "Bird flu. It would impact everything and you can't prepare."

- Sergey Brin, co-founder, Google: "The environment and escalating disasters."

It's striking how much focus was on external calamity, as if terrorism and avian flu were the only forces capable of halting the phenomenal tide of growth and prosperity. The only one of so many I interviewed who said anything about banks being at risk was Deutsche Bank CEO Josef Ackermann. In reply to my question, he said, "Overleveraging in the real estate market." *Bingo!* He got it. (Years later I asked Ackermann how he had been so prescient, and he told me that he would advise anyone who asked him that the two biggest problems to avoid in any successful economy were indebtedness and real estate bubbles. When I asked, "So, did you do anything about it?" he admitted, "We did a little, not a lot," noting how competitive the market was then and how difficult it is to put the brakes on during a boom.)

———

In January 2007 I conducted another interview with David Rubenstein of the Carlyle Group. "What are your expectations for the year? Can this keep up?" I asked him. Rubenstein answered, "It's hard to believe it can get any better." He said that assuming there was no cataclysmic event like 9/11, he expected 2007 to be another big year.

That prediction, born of what—false optimism, bravado, blindness, deceit?—did not come true. Within weeks of Rubenstein's remark, the gloom was setting in. It was going to be a very long year, and a very long fall to earth. This is the story of that fall.

ONE

Nightmare on Liberty Street

"Because of what he did with Bear Stearns, everybody thought good ol' Hank [Paulson] would be there with the money."
—A FORMER TREASURY DEPARTMENT OFFICIAL,
IN AN INTERVIEW WITH MARIA BARTIROMO

SEPTEMBER 12, 2008

The Federal Reserve Bank of New York rises up from a narrow street in the financial district of Manhattan, a literal fortress of limestone and sandstone whose cavernous subterranean vault houses 25 percent of the world's gold supply. The building is a commanding emblem of the security and size of the American economy, and few people enter its Liberty Street doors without feeling a power surge. When times are flush, they may even have an exhilarated spring to their step, happy to be at the center of prosperity. But the men who streamed out of the line of black cars on Liberty Street in the waning afternoon hours of Friday, September 12, 2008, did so with heads bent, battling gusting winds and a torrential downpour. To a man they were extremely grim. Their names were among Wall

Street's elite—Jamie Dimon, of JPMorgan Chase; Vikram Pandit, of Citigroup; Brady Dougan, of Credit Suisse; John Thain, now of Merrill Lynch; John Mack, of Morgan Stanley; Lloyd Blankfein, of Goldman Sachs; Robert Kelly, of Bank of New York Mellon; and Robert Wolf, of UBS Group. Waiting inside were the horsemen of the apocalypse—or, perhaps, the angels of salvation (no one knew then which it would be)—Treasury secretary Henry "Hank" Paulson, New York Fed president Timothy Geithner, and SEC chairman Christopher Cox. At issue that particular day was the fate of Lehman Brothers, the 158-year-old investment banking firm that formed one of the pillars of Wall Street. The men gathering faced the blunt reality that Lehman could not open for business the following Monday without a rescue—and that rescue was in their hands.

As the titans of capitalism plowed through the rain-drenched streets of lower Manhattan, each was filled with a deep inner turmoil. Several of them would later admit to me how troubled they were. John Mack, CEO of Morgan Stanley, who had earned the nickname "Mack the Knife" for his ruthless, unsentimental ability to slash costs and pursue profits, spoke softly as he recalled the sense of crisis. "The dominoes were falling," he said, "and one of them was almost Morgan Stanley." Every man present was likely feeling the same way—not just concern for Lehman, but dreading his own fate.

The meeting was called for 6:00 p.m., but the bad weather delayed it until nearly 7:00. Rain always means traffic bottlenecks in New York, especially on a Friday night. Mack described the ride down from the Morgan Stanley offices in midtown. "It was pouring, and traffic was stopped. I was worried that we wouldn't get there on time. And my driver, who was an ex-policeman, said, 'Hey, boss, do you see that bike lane over there? Does it go all the way down to the

Battery?' I said, 'Yeah, I think it does.' So we took the bike lane and got there in five minutes. That's how important it seemed."

Hank Paulson and a couple of associates had flown in from Washington, and their car crawled through the clogged streets. While he rode, Paulson worked the phone. For more than a week he had been trying to facilitate a behind-the-scenes deal with Lehman Brothers and one of two promising suitors—Bank of America and the British bank Barclays. It was no secret that BofA was the preferred buyer. Certainly, Lehman CEO Dick Fuld felt that way, and many others shared the view that the company should be kept in American hands. Earlier that day Paulson had taken a call from New York senator Chuck Schumer, expressing concern about the prospect of the Brits buying Lehman. He suggested that a foreign owner wouldn't have the same commitment to jobs as an American firm, and he worried about setting off a firing spree on Wall Street.

Like a manic marriage broker, Paulson had been going back and forth between Fuld and Bank of America's CEO, Ken Lewis. Paulson knew that after JPMorgan acquired Bear Stearns earlier that year, Bank of America was likely the strongest, most deep-pocketed American bank that could pull off another takeover. Lewis was attracted to the idea of buying Lehman, with one big caveat: he wanted to leave behind the toxic assets—that is, those whose value had declined so substantially that they represented a burden on the balance sheet. It was like making an offer to buy a house except for the leaking roof. Paulson stated repeatedly that the federal government was not going to be on the hook for the bad assets. A private-sector solution was required. But Ken Lewis didn't seem to register what Paulson was saying. Now, sitting in his car, Paulson took another call from Lewis.

"Okay, I'll do a deal if you guarantee all the bad assets."

Paulson sighed heavily. "Ken, we can't do that."

"Then I'm out," Lewis said.

Paulson urged him to wait. He told him about the meeting at the Federal Reserve and suggested that perhaps a consortium of banks could get together and take on some of Lehman's toxicity. Lewis agreed to hold off on a decision, but he didn't sound optimistic.

"Do you think he's really serious about buying Lehman?" Paulson's chief of staff, Jim Wilkinson, asked. They were all beginning to have their doubts. Separate conversations were being held with Barclays, just in case. Members of Paulson's staff were constantly on the phone with the British regulators who, like Lewis, were balking at the idea of taking on Lehman's debt. It was going to be a long weekend, and Paulson had no idea going in whether they'd be able to pull off the save.

I remember asking someone from the Treasury that week whether Lehman's toxic assets were so much worse than what anybody else had on the books.

"Oh, yeah," he said. "The difference between Bear and Lehman was that everybody had been into Lehman looking at its books. They knew exactly how bad it was. I was in there with Bank of America, and they were talking about just some of this horrible land. Believe me, it was awful."

———

Contrary to the way it is portrayed in movies, the floor of the New York Stock Exchange is not consumed by frenzy or populated by unruly, shouting traders. Computers long ago replaced ticker tape, and the scene today is of hundreds of people hunched over their terminals making electronic trades. Even so, a visceral energy pulses through the vast room. When the opening bell rings each morning at 9:30, no one can predict with any certainty how the market is going to end at 4:00 p.m.—although hundreds of analysts and reporters are dedicated to the job of divining the outcome. I have been reporting from the floor for more than fifteen years. My afternoon show, *Closing Bell*, broadcasts between 3:00 and 5:00 p.m., which is the apex of global trading. And during this particular time, the nervousness was surreal. Every day I would come in not knowing what to expect. We would watch massive gyrations with the Dow, down 500, 600, 700 points on some days and up 500 points on others. Investors were nervous, and the nervousness manifested itself on markets around the world.

Closing Bell focuses on the financial issues everyone is talking about, and during the few days leading up to that "big weekend," the talk was about Lehman Brothers: Would it survive until Monday? How much did it matter to the financial health of Wall Street if Lehman went down? Would the Fed backstop a purchase as it had done with Bear Stearns six months earlier? Were there serious suitors that might rescue Lehman? The experts were generally pessimistic about Lehman, and the flashing board told the tale: the once-great investment firm's stock closed on Friday at a paltry $3 a share, down from a fifty-two-week high of $67.73.

To outsiders, the crisis might have seemed sudden, shocking, unbelievable—a bolt from nowhere. But it had been coming for a long time. A Lehman insider, recalling the months leading up to this fateful moment, told me, "By Friday, September 12, we just wanted to get through the damn day. Every day you'd sit there and think 'I can't wait until the market closes.' People were transfixed by the ticker and what was happening to our stock price." Now months of agony and hope were coming to a final reckoning, and the actions of the men gathering at the Fed would define the financial landscape for years and even decades to come.

By the time I arrived at the New York Stock Exchange for *Closing Bell* on Friday, I had been working the phones and text messaging for hours. Lehman Brothers was on the ropes. With the announcement of third-quarter losses of nearly $4 billion, credit agencies were threatening a downgrade unless Lehman raised substantial cash before the weekend was out. Share prices had plummeted throughout the week. Rumors had been floating around for weeks that the state-owned Korea Development Bank (KDB) was talking about acquiring Lehman and/or taking a sizable stake, but that deal was dead by the weekend. My sources told me that the Koreans had made an offer of capital in exchange for a 50 percent stake, but Fuld declined it. "It's not enough," he told them, asking for much more than they wanted to pay. He overreached and lost the deal.

Midway through my show, my BlackBerry started buzzing with the news that Tim Geithner had called a major-league powwow for later that evening, and the principals of the big firms were heading down to the Federal Reserve.

Not everyone knew the exact reason for the summons, but when Geithner called, they responded. The head of the New York Federal Reserve had that power.

"Tell me what's happening," I said to one of my sources. He laughed. "Let's put it this way," he said. "The call from Geithner wasn't a request. He didn't say 'Would you mind coming down?' It was more like an order."

"Is it about Lehman?" I asked.

"I think so," he replied. "I think they're going to try and get a pound of flesh from us." He said he expected Geithner and Paulson to pressure the firms to ante up some hard cash to save Lehman.

Moments later, I was back on air, fielding a series of commentators, lining up for an anticipated weekend bloodbath around Lehman Brothers. By now it had become somewhat commonplace to wait for the weekend meetings to get news before the opening of the Asian markets on Sunday. This weekend felt the same, but it was actually more significant. "The world changed very quickly and caught the U.S. financial system off guard," Mohamed El-Erian told me, adding, "When we look back we're going to say, 'Wow! That was a period when the U.S. financial system was redefined.'"

With Lehman shares at rock bottom as we neared the close, everyone was speculating about what price Lehman might command, and whether there were any viable suitors. There was broad agreement that Lehman was *not* too big to fail. "They have their hat in their hand at this point," said David Kelly of JPMorgan. Harvard University professor Martin Feldstein agreed that Lehman was no Bear Stearns and probably did not warrant a government backstop. "There is no reason why the shareholders or, indeed, the creditors of Lehman should be protected if in fact there isn't enough capital there for Lehman to be viable," he said. Feldstein was joining a growing chorus of financial experts who believed the system had reached a dangerous tipping point of too much government involvement, brought about by an overleveraged system. But there was still debate about whether the firm would, in fact, be forced to declare bankruptcy.

Jerry Webman, chief economist at Oppenheimer Funds, voiced deep concern. "This is a sea change in the financial world," he said on my show that day. "For twenty-five years we've had an economy based on financial leverage—earnings based on the ability to borrow and put borrowing on top of borrowing, easy money driving these economies, driving earnings forward. What we're trying to do right now is sort out who's got a good long-term earnings model from solid business and whose balance sheet is potentially a lot of air."

Most people I spoke with said to me, "Maria, this is different. This is unbelievable. This is the worst thing I've ever seen." And it wasn't just the specter of a bunch of wealthy Wall Streeters being toppled. Unlike Bear Stearns, where stock in the company was mostly held by the top executives, Lehman had a trickle-down ownership culture, with the lower rungs of the company, such as executive assistants, paid in stock. If Lehman fell, there would be a lot of average people left with nothing.

As the business day drew to a close, CNBC showed scenes of Lehman employees leaving the building, saying that they didn't know if they would be back Monday. There were many tear-streaked faces outside Lehman headquarters in Times Square that day. Even so, few people, including the principals, believed Lehman would go down. For those on the outside, it was simply inconceivable.

———

The three men on the hot seat this weekend—Tim Geithner, Hank Paulson, and Chris Cox—were by no means a cookie-cutter team of financial types. That is to say, these were bright and very different men who shared one big commonality: the desire to get something important accomplished, popularity be damned. There are few times in life when one's actions may create history, and they all knew that this was one of them.

New York Fed president Tim Geithner took a lot of ribbing for his youthfulness. The first time people met the slender forty-seven-year-old, they often remarked that he looked too green to bear such a large responsibility. The word most often used to describe him was "boyish." But Geithner's résumé was impressive. Born in New York City, the second-generation offspring of German immigrants, Geithner spent most of his childhood living abroad and graduated from Dartmouth with a degree in Asian studies.

One thing that distinguished Geithner was that he wasn't a product of Wall Street. His rabbi was former Treasury secretary Robert Rubin, who years earlier told me, "Geithner will one day be Treasury secretary." When he was tapped for the Fed position in 2003, Geithner was working at the Council on Foreign Relations, and, indeed, he'd spent his entire career in government and quasi-government positions. He didn't come from the culture of the Street, where success was often measured in sizable bonuses and fat stock portfolios. He and his wife and two children lived in a modest house in Westchester County and were not regulars on the New York social scene. (Later, when Geithner was named Treasury secretary by Barack Obama, he had a tough time selling his house, even after he'd slashed the price to under $1 million. He eventually rented it while he waited for the real estate market to turn around.)

Geithner's low-key, no-drama style was well suited to his position. But no one ever accused Geithner of being a pushover.

In a crisis, Geithner made a good partner for Paulson, who was known to be emotional and passionate. In office just under two years, Paulson brought almost a religious fervor to his job; he felt he was there for a purpose.

Unlike Geithner, Paulson was the epitome of a Wall Street man. Before President Bush nominated him for the Treasury, he was the chairman and CEO of Goldman Sachs, a firm he had joined back in 1974.

A Christian Scientist and a family man, he was a quiet, though influential, player in corporate America long before becoming secretary.

Paulson's job, arriving at the Fed, was to convince the CEOs that the solution was up to them. "Everyone thought good ol' Hank would be there with the money as he was with Bear Stearns," a source at the Treasury told me. "And they weren't going to believe otherwise until Hank told them in person."

In truth, the federal government did not have the authority to lend money to failing institutions, only to institutions that were solvent. The reason a Bear Stearns backstop had been possible in March was because a highly solvent institution, JPMorgan, took over. The Fed could not have loaned money to Bear Stearns directly, but it was able to do so with JPMorgan's help. Paulson was essentially paving the way for a similar setup with Lehman Brothers and a solvent savior such as Bank of America or Barclays—with one difference. He wanted the backstop to come from the private sector.

The third man on the team, Christopher Cox, was the "grim reaper." His primary task was to shepherd Lehman Brothers through a bankruptcy proceeding, if that was to become necessary. At fifty-five, Cox had worn many hats in his career, including a stint at the Reagan White House and seventeen years as a California congressman. The accomplishments of his professional life were set against the backdrop of remarkable personal crises that underscored his ability to make a comeback. In 1978 he was paralyzed from the waist down in an off-road Jeep accident. He eventually regained the use of his legs, though he was often in pain, even thirty years later. Then, shortly after he became SEC chairman, Cox was diagnosed with cancer. He battled the illness while maintaining a heavy work schedule, and by 2008 was deemed fully recovered.

But while there was much to admire about Cox personally, a chorus of criticism followed him throughout 2008. As the government's primary watchdog, the SEC looked ineffectual in its failure to spot the looming crisis and prevent it. As he joined Geithner and Paulson at the Federal Reserve, Cox had to know his reputation was on the line.

———

The CEOs were sitting around a long table in the conference room on the first floor when Paulson, Geithner, and Cox walked in. The mood was restless and uncertain. These men were not accustomed to collaborating, and while the call to do so was not completely unprecedented, it wasn't something you'd see in other industries. Imagine, for example, General Motors and Ford being pressured to save Chrysler, or NBC and Fox forking over the funds to save CBS. It just wouldn't happen. But the financial industry was more interrelated. One drowning company could sink them all. Faced with that reality, they had to put aside their modus operandi—to try to kill one another—and start to work together.

Ironically, the last time the Wall Street companies had been called upon to rescue one of their own, Lehman Brothers had been deeply involved as well. It was 1998. Robert Rubin was Treasury secretary, William McDonough was New York Fed president, and Dick Fuld was four years into his tenure as Lehman CEO. A giant hedge fund called Long-Term Capital Management was on the brink of collapse, having lost $4.6 billion in the space of a few months. Since most of the Wall Street firms had ties to Long-Term Capital, the Federal Reserve feared that a failure would have a traumatic ripple effect. In particular, Lehman was vulnerable. The Wall Street firms got together in a consortium and put their money on the table. Several firms pledged $300 million each, including Barclays, Chase, Goldman Sachs, Merrill Lynch, Morgan Stanley, and JPMorgan. Fuld pledged $100 million on behalf of Lehman, saying he couldn't afford to do more. Long-Term Capital Management was saved, and Fuld got a lot of credit within his own company for bringing Lehman back from the brink. Notably, Jimmy Cayne at Bear Stearns refused to give any money, irking his colleagues.

Geithner opened the meeting. In his quiet, unemotional voice he laid out a gloom-and-doom scenario of what a Lehman fall might mean for the rest of them. Paulson spoke second, telling the men flat out that he didn't have the legal authority to save Lehman. That was up to the people around the table. Initially, there was push back. Wasn't there something the feds could do, without having to rely on the banks for a rescue? But very soon these men, who were top professionals, pivoted and said, "Okay, how can we manage this?" They had all done deals with Hank Paulson in the past, and one thing they knew about him was that when he said "We're not bailing Lehman out" he meant it. Paulson never showed his gun without using it.

Chris Cox spoke last, describing how the SEC would manage a bankruptcy, if one were to happen. No one wanted to go there, but it was Cox's job to take them if necessary.

Although all the news and theorizing were about Lehman, Fuld was nowhere to be seen. He wasn't invited to the Fed because the discussions were about him and his firm. But that didn't mean there wasn't a lot of speculation about what he was up to. Moody, passionate, and proprietary about his company, Fuld was fully engaged on the thirty-first floor of the Lehman Brothers building at the top of Times Square. His lieutenants were at his side, trying to work every last-minute angle. Those close to Fuld said that he believed with all his heart that if things turned bad they could orchestrate a deal similar to that of Bear Stearns. It never occurred to anyone, least of all Fuld, that the government would not be there to catch Lehman if it fell. An aura of denial filled Lehman's executive suite in the period leading up to the end.

Behind the drama being played out on Liberty Street and in midtown Manhattan was a fact few people realized. There was some personal animosity between Paulson and Fuld, based on their different backgrounds and temperaments. Paulson was a lifetime investment banker; Fuld was a lifetime commercial paper trader. A source told me of a dinner between the two men in the spring of 2008. "A lot of people in the press thought it was a warm and fuzzy dinner," he said. "But it was actually very intense. At one point Dick Fuld lectured Hank Paulson, saying, 'I've been in my seat a lot longer than you've been in yours. Don't tell me how to do my job.'" How ironic that a few months later, Fuld would be so reliant on Paulson's good graces.

Even before it reached full-crisis mode, Lehman had developed a credibility problem, and everyone in the room knew it. I, too, had been hearing the whispers for months. Larry McDonald, who was a vice president and a trader at the firm until 2008, did not mince words when he spoke to me of his former company; no question that as a "worker bee" at the firm, McDonald had an ax to grind. He had become one of the harshest critics of Lehman's culture, even writing a book about it in 2009—*A Colossal Failure of Common Sense*. His view was not unbiased, but it did show how embattled many people down the ranks were feeling at Lehman during that period.

"There was a disconnect between the men in the ivory tower and the wonderful people who worked at the firm," he told me. "Lehman Brothers, to me, was never rotten at the core. That's where all the beauty was. It was rotten at the head. There was so much talent in the middle that tried to stop the madness. One by one, those who spoke up were silenced. At Lehman, you kept your head down and you did your job, or you lost both."

McDonald painted a picture of a fiefdom where those in the royal suites were more interested in the aura of their personal wealth than the health of the company, and he said that this was especially true at the seat of power—the thirty-first floor of the Lehman building. "The thirty-first floor is one of the most mysterious places on earth," McDonald confided to me. "Some people claim it resembles a Sotheby's art collection facility—or a cross between that and a human resources pom-pom bonfire festival. You had people up there who were totally distanced from the trading floor, very concerned about their new memberships in the billionaires' club—or I should say the $200 billion art club." (In fairness, the space, including the art collection, was not unlike those of most Wall Street firms, but if viewed through a prism of disappointment and resentment, the lavish atmosphere might grate.)

McDonald claimed that Fuld took his eye off the ball years before the collapse, while many in the lower echelons of the company were issuing dire warnings. "As early as 2006, some of the most talented people at Lehman wanted us out of the subprime mortgage business," he said. "We started seeing weird things happening—such as people missing their *first* mortgage payments. That was unprecedented. There was something wrong. It was like a slow-motion car wreck."

Certainly, Fuld had his defenders at the firm. "To say Dick was not engaged is nonsense," one of them told me. "Leading up to mid-September, he was working around the clock to save the firm. And he was getting absolutely no help from the SEC in dealing with the shorts and the rumors, or from other banks. Look at JPMorgan. They were the bank that facilitated Lehman's trades. There's a clause in the contract that basically gives them the right to ask for however much collateral they want. So they just started grabbing more and more and more collateral. And it was devastating."

———

Robert Diamond was not a particularly emotional guy. His long face was pleasant but inscrutable. The president of British-owned Barclays Capital was known to be a cagey player, with the placid air common to members of large families. One of seven children, Diamond grew up in Concord, Massachusetts. Both of his parents were schoolteachers. Although Barclays was Britain's premiere bank, Diamond retained an abiding love and loyalty for the home teams—the New England Patriots and the Boston Red Sox. He was, beneath the British flag, a quintessential Wall Street guy, who had cut his teeth at Morgan Stanley and had joined Barclays only after being passed over for the top job there.

On Friday, September 12, Diamond's normally calm demeanor was shaken by the weight of phenomenal responsibility. He felt uncommonly emotional as he sat in a room on the fourth floor of the Federal Reserve, away from the main conference room where the CEOs were gathered. Diamond thought that he, in particular, was on the line because many people were looking to his company to rescue Lehman, and he just didn't know if it could be done.

For more than a year Barclays had been actively pursuing growth in the United States, looking for the right vehicle. After the Bear Stearns fire sale, it occurred to Diamond that perhaps it could be the template for a deal, and the firm that came to mind was Lehman Brothers. He thought, "What an incredible opportunity." He salivated thinking about Lehman's thirty-two-story building and its ten thousand New York employees. But he wanted a distress price, and he wanted a government backstop—just like Jamie Dimon of JPMorgan got for Bear Stearns earlier in the year.

Diamond had many unofficial conversations with Hank Paulson and his people as the summer stretched into fall. These were "what if" discussions as Diamond felt his way on matters of procedure and price. In the days before the final weekend, the discussions intensified. Thursday, September 11, a team from Barclays had begun doing their due diligence, taking apart Lehman's books, and they would continue, sleepless, throughout the weekend.

"It was clear to us that this was a fantastic franchise," Diamond recalled to me. "The scope of its business was impressive and many were operating very well." But the drawbacks were just as striking, and they all boiled down to one reality: Lehman had no liquidity.

Now Diamond was feeling the stress. He was not a poker player, and this was a beads-of-sweat-inducing moment. "It was stressful. It was emotional," he told me later. "We realized we were playing for big stakes. So, on one hand, we knew that if Lehman went into bankruptcy, there would be huge implications in the market. On the other hand, we wanted to look at whether or not there was a transaction that made sense for Barclays, as well as for the markets."

The problem: Hank Paulson's insistence that there would be no federal backstop, no bailout, no sweet Bear-style deal. Bob Diamond wanted Lehman. But could it happen? Would his own regulator, Britain's Financial Services Authority, allow a sale?

John Thain had been riding high for some time. His career was on a fast track. He was savvy and cerebral, with a square jaw and a bland demeanor, and a résumé that was rock solid. Thain had been president and co-chief operating officer at Goldman Sachs before becoming CEO of the New York Stock Exchange. He had held the top job at Merrill Lynch for only nine months. When he was brought in to replace the retiring chief executive, Stan O'Neal, everyone on Wall Street had been surprised. The scuttlebutt was that Thain would be tapped to replace Chuck Prince at Citigroup and that Larry Fink of BlackRock would take over Merrill. But I was told that Fink would not entertain the idea unless he was allowed to review Merrill's balance sheet and accounting, a reasonable request that the board denied. So Thain was the choice. He was hired to strengthen a rudderless company, as he told me in November 2007 when he started his new job. "The board is looking for leadership," he said. "The board is looking for strategy and direction. The board is looking to unify the company."

From the outset Thain was aggressive in his efforts to strengthen Merrill. His first task was to get rid of the bad assets on Merrill's books. He brought in highly paid, talented executives—many of them former colleagues from Goldman Sachs. Among them was a top examiner whom he paid $40 million to clean up the books. Hearing about the exorbitant number, I asked Thain, "Is it true? How do you justify bringing this guy over and paying him so much?" Thain defended the idea. "That's right," he said. "I'm going to pay him. He's a talented guy, and I am going to pay top dollar to ensure this never happens again." It was a huge payday for the examiner, who wound up staying three months.

Now, sitting at the Fed, Thain listened carefully to what was being said. For Thain and his colleagues it was glaringly apparent that much more was at stake than just the future of Lehman Brothers. This was a massive wake-up call, a thump on the head to all the Wall Street firms. It was no longer about one firm failing—be it Bear Stearns or Lehman—it was about the tangled interconnectivity. The major Wall Street firms were like climbers roped together on an icy slope. Earlier that day, Merrill's board of directors had a conference call with Thain expressing concerns that the short-sellers would be coming after Merrill next. No one was immune. "I'd better figure out how to protect Merrill," he thought, "or we could be next." Although Thain had assured his board that Merrill was no Lehman, he could envision a similar downward spiral occurring, especially if the short-sellers set their sights on his firm, creating a run on the bank.

Paulson and Geithner were pushing the top firms to share the burden. Politically, Paulson didn't think he could save another Wall Street firm. There was too much pressure, especially from Republicans in Washington, to not bail out anybody else. He wanted the rescue, if there were to be one, to come from Lehman's counterparts.

"We have to figure out what needs to be done here," Paulson told them. He outlined the options, including potential mergers. Lloyd Blankfein, CEO of Goldman Sachs, thought things were moving a little too fast. "All right," he said, preparing to leave, "let me think about this and I'll get back to you. I have to speak to my board."

"Yeah, you can think about it," Paulson replied, pointing in the direction of meeting rooms down the hall. "Take a room. We're going to fix it this weekend. You're not going anywhere. If you need to talk to your boards and bosses, you'll have privacy. But we're doing it this weekend, before the Asian markets open Sunday night."

Morgan Stanley's John Mack sat gloomily at the table, feeling that the March sale of Bear Stearns had been a dress rehearsal for the big show that was now happening before him. He had spoken to Dick Fuld on several occasions in recent months, trying to figure out if there were things that could be done—assets that could be purchased, even a merger. But nothing was clicking. "You had this sense," he told me later, "that we were all tracked for some change, especially Lehman. What that meeting brought to the forefront was the reality of it and the impact of it. I don't think we fully understood until then how bad it really was. The question was, how did you contain this contagion? Could you build a buffer that stopped with Lehman?"

Mack contemplated the possibility that the markets really could melt down. He didn't feel scared, but the determination was growing in him, and he could see it in others around the table. They *had* to fix this problem.

Robert Wolf, chairman and CEO of UBS Group, had received the call from Geithner's office at 3:30, saying, "Please come down. There's going to be a meeting." He replied, "Can you tell me what this is in reference to?" The person on the line wasn't too forthcoming except to say, "If you need to invite someone, I'd recommend bringing your chief risk officer."

Wolf chuckled, remembering the call. "Obviously, some people were more in the loop than I was, because they'd been engaged earlier by the Fed or by Lehman."

Citigroup CEO Vikram Pandit was not entirely clear why he had been summoned to the Federal Reserve, but he could feel the buzzing sense of urgency as soon as he arrived. Pandit had joined Citi in 2007 when it acquired his hedge fund, Old Lane Partners, for $800 million, and almost immediately got bumped up to the top position after Chuck Prince was forced to resign. Now, sitting across the table from

Paulson and Geithner, surrounded by his peers, he sensed the dread in the room. This wasn't just about one company, he realized.

Prior to that day, there had been a lot of argument over possible solutions—government assistance, buyouts, and mergers. But on Friday, September 12, it sank in that a Lehman bankruptcy would have ripple effects, and the key players realized they needed to stop bickering and try to figure out answers.

One observer painted a remarkable picture for me of powerful opponents working together. "I looked at Jamie Dimon sitting across from Lloyd Blankfein, and I thought I'd love to write a book called *Lloyd Blankfein vs. Jamie Dimon*," he said. "Those two were the giants in the room, and they hated each other so much it was impossible to believe they were sitting there. But you know what? They were very good, very willing to cooperate. And through the whole process I thought Jamie Dimon came off looking better than anybody. He was the guy that always rose above the pettiness with common sense and good ideas." He was also the one who probably knew more than the others, being the healthiest bank at the table. No surprise later when his competitors railed at him for turning up the screws and demanding more collateral just when it hurt the most.

The men at the Fed working on the Lehman crisis had been divided into three groups. The first group was tasked with examining Lehman's financials and determining how much capital would be needed. The second group was assigned to figure out a rescue structure. And the third group was assigned to figure out what would happen if Lehman could not be saved. "You've got to try harder," Geithner warned them, his temper frayed. They seethed—no one appreciated being lectured to by Geithner. But they went off to their groups to get started.

TWO

The Bubble Machine

"Although a 'bubble' in home prices for the nation as a whole does not appear likely, there do appear to be, at a minimum, signs of froth in some local markets where home prices seem to have risen to unsustainable levels."
—ALAN GREENSPAN, TESTIFYING BEFORE CONGRESS, JUNE 9, 2005

The most common question people ask me, looking back on the financial meltdown of September 2008 from the perspective of 2010, is, "How did it happen?" How could the financial markets go from such euphoric highs to such desperate lows? And where were the guardians at the gates—those investment banking geniuses with their perfect instincts and fat bonuses who were supposed to predict trouble and make course corrections? Where were the congressional watchdogs on Capitol Hill or the regulators at the SEC? There were some skeptics, hedge funds that resisted the euphoria and bet against the boom and made huge profits. There were some worrisome signs, but only in retrospect did we understand the systemic nature of the crisis. However, there is no question that the tsunami that hit Wall Street started with a trickle of unconventional mortgage loans that nobody imagined could mean such big trouble.

The euphoria of the housing-boom years was intoxicating, and it fueled a sense of urgency with a pulsing mantra: *Buy, buy, buy!* Home ownership had always been a cornerstone of the American dream, but in the past it was possible only for those who fit certain criteria. Everyone understood that in order to qualify for a home mortgage you had to have a secure job with an income that could comfortably accommodate a monthly mortgage payment, a good credit rating, and a cash down payment of 10 to 20 percent of the purchase price. But fueled by low interest rates and a booming housing market, nonbanks started getting in on the mortgage action. These entities were not as strictly regulated as conventional banks, and soon the mortgage business became tainted as brokers dropped the qualification standards and began writing loans for people with poor credit who couldn't come up with down payments. They were dubbed "liar loans" because they required practically no verification. You could have claimed to be the Queen of England and walked away with a loan and a "Thank you, Ma'am" without a second look. We all remember the commercials touting the miraculous news: nothing down, no credit check, no requirements, everybody qualifies. It seemed too good to be true, and it was. Usually, subprime mortgages were pumped-up versions of adjustable rate mortgages (ARMs). That is, the interest rates were very low or nonexistent in the early years but then were adjusted to a much higher rate later on. The effect was that monthly mortgage payments shot up; some even doubled. The bitter irony of the setup was that subprime borrowers were the least able to withstand a sudden financial hit.

By 2007 large numbers of borrowers were facing default as the terms of their loans reset, and they were no longer able to afford their monthly payments. Massive defaults put a strain on lenders, but the fallout went far beyond them. By the time the subprime defaults began to pile up, the risk had imbedded itself into the financial system, through mortgage-backed securities.

Mortgage-backed securities are debt obligations on mortgage loans, which are purchased from banks or mortgage companies. During the height of the mortgage boom, investment banks started devising innovative "products"—in particular, the means of packaging subprime mortgages into securities that would be sold to other investment banks and presented to investors. These mortgage securities were quite lucrative when times were good, but when people began defaulting on their loans, the securities plummeted in value. The concept of mortgage-backed securities was originally developed by Lewis Ranieri, a Salomon Brothers bond trader, in the 1980s. During his career, Ranieri received wide acclaim for the concept, which produced huge profits for Wall Street.

Major investment banks were caught holding the bag—billions of dollars worth of so-called tier-three assets, the riskiest mortgage assets. Quarter after quarter, investment banks were forced to take write-downs against earnings. But even huge write-downs weren't enough because the market never loosened up. No one wanted mortgage securities anymore.

In retrospect, the fact that so few people saw the danger building during the boom years is remarkable. There are many explanations for why this is so. Ed Lazear was an insider throughout the panic, as chairman of President Bush's Economic Council. (He'd replaced Ben Bernanke in 2006, when Bernanke became chairman of the Fed.) "It's not that events like this hadn't happened before," he said, "but events of this magnitude had not happened before. So if you look at the housing data you'll see a nearly uninterrupted pattern of housing-price increases. And it wasn't like these guys were fools. They were performing stress tests; they were doing analysis. But their models were based on the historical precedent, and, unfortunately, we hadn't seen an event like this historically. When they set up their models and asked what were the right numbers, the right parameters, these were not the ranges we saw in this particular collapse."

That was all well and good, but on the ground, people were struggling to get their heads around such a devastating failure on the part of those who were supposed to know better. Lazear recalled that he saw it frequently. "When I was working at the White House, I used to commute home to California every second or third weekend," he said. "So I was on planes a lot. And I always talked to the flight attendants because flight attendants know everything. They're like the cab drivers of the air. They're in touch with people. So I was talking to this one flight attendant, and he was disgusted, saying, 'I can't understand how people could be so stupid. They're making these loans to these guys who have no income, no jobs, no ability to pay. That's totally nuts. Any idiot could see it.' And my answer was that he was right. Any idiot *could* see it, and, in fact, the market saw it. That's why it was called *subprime*. And so it wasn't that these guys didn't see it. They surely saw it. They understood that the default risk was much higher on those loans, and that's why the interest rates were also much higher. What they didn't see was that the default rates would be significantly higher."

I got his point, but all explanations seemed feeble. One thing was unmistakable: By 2007, the boom times were effectively drawing to an end. No more lavish parties. No more euphoria. It was Judgment Day.

———

Angelo Mozilo was never one to show fear. I interviewed the chairman of Countrywide Financial on several occasions during 2007, and he was determinedly optimistic, as if by force of personality and will he could halt the rapid decline of Countrywide's stock. Mozilo, the rough-hewn son of a butcher from the Bronx, had started the company in 1969, and by 2007 it was the largest lender in America, with sixty-two thousand employees and nine hundred offices. Mozilo was the king of home loans, and during the phenomenal housing boom, being number one also meant doing substantial business in subprime loans. As one investor remarked to me, "Mozilo was the Crazy Eddie of the housing market. No deal was impossible. He was *giving it away.*" He wasn't, of course, giving it away. Over a period of years, as the fees multiplied and the ARMs came due, these were extremely lucrative loans, far more so than conventional mortgages— until they began to default in high numbers.

When I spoke with Mozilo in March 2007, as the cracks were starting to appear in the real estate industry, he was on the defensive, feeling misunderstood and wrongly targeted. Like some of his counterparts, he was quick to blame the media for creating the aura of crisis where he felt none existed. "It's distressing to me to see the piling on that's taking place by the media and regulators," he complained. "This was a system that was working very well, providing an opportunity for people to get over that barrier of entry to owning a home. Now what you have is panic setting in."

But the system was hardly "working very well" by that time. I pointed out to Mozilo that it wasn't the *media* that was to blame for an epidemic of home foreclosures. Mozilo brushed me off. Throughout our interview he touted his company's affinity for the little guy with aspirations of home ownership. The question was, could the little guy afford the loan that Countrywide and other lenders were selling him? "Countrywide for forty years has been on a mission to lower the barriers of entry for the American people to have the opportunity of home ownership," he said with emotion. "And every application we take is within that framework of making certain as best we can that these individuals can afford the home. And so my response is simply that we have not been an opportunist, but have created opportunities for individuals and families to own a home."

It was true that Mozilo was helping to open up home ownership to a broad range of people. The question was, should they have had this opportunity if they did not have the means to be homeowners?

Was Mozilo putting a bright spin on a troubling situation? A later investigation uncovered e-mails that suggested Mozilo knew his lending program was deeply, even fatally, flawed. An April 17, 2006, e-mail, uncovered by federal investigators in 2009, found Mozilo complaining to Countrywide president David Sambol about the subprime lending program:

> In all my years in the business I have never seen a more toxic product. . . . With real estate values coming down . . . the product will become increasingly worse. There has to be major

changes in this program, including substantial increases in the minimum FICO.

So, although Mozilo knew back in 2006 that the subprime loans were, in his word, "toxic," he was still defending them in 2007. He insisted that Countrywide did not arrange loans for unqualified buyers. He took a blame-the-victim approach, saying that no one forced consumers to sign up for the risky adjustable rate mortgages. Yet by the time we spoke a second time, in August 2007, almost one in four subprime loans that Countrywide serviced was delinquent. Critics were saying that Countrywide was determined to write mortgages at any cost—and while they weren't alone in that, they were out in front. Ignoring the fault lines in his own company, Mozilo boasted to me that Countrywide would actually be a beneficiary of the subprime crisis, because all the bad players (presumably the competition) would be forced out of the lending business. He even spun a $2 billion cash infusion from Bank of America that summer as a sign of Countrywide's strength. "We had a lot of people approach us over the months [wanting to invest], but Bank of America is the best—a marquee name. There's only one Bank of America. For them to attach themselves to Countrywide is priceless."

"Yes," I pressed, a bit puzzled, "but why would they *not* want to do it? Look at the terms." BofA's stock purchase valued Countrywide at a paltry $18 a share. "Let's face it, Angelo, people are saying, 'Sure, it's great for Bank of America, but the terms are not great for Countrywide.'"

"Yeah, they're great for Countrywide," Mozilo protested. "They're fantastic for Countrywide!"

It didn't help Mozilo's case that he was busy dumping his own stock—reportedly $140 million worth in a matter of months. I asked him, "Don't you worry that shareholders will say, 'He's selling. He must be losing confidence. Maybe I should sell?'" The suggestion angered him. "As a CEO, the only way to eliminate that issue is to never sell stock, just die. Die owning stock," he snapped. He felt it was perfectly acceptable for a CEO to diversify and to cash in. That may have been true, but he ignored how the timing of the sale was sure to raise eyebrows.

By December, with conditions continuing to worsen, Mozilo was a bit chastened but still undaunted. He told me in an emotional statement, "Every day I'd wake up and say, 'Okay, we're through that problem.' And then I'd go to work around four in the morning, and there was another problem, two problems, three problems. It was incredible because it began feeding itself. And what I've found out in this process—because I've never been through anything like this before—I've been through a lot in fifty-five years, but nothing like this—is that people are lemmings. They just keep on attacking because fear sets in. And everybody's fearful. 'I don't want to be the last one left behind in this burning house, so I'm going to get out of here.'" He was angry at the media's role in raising the alarm. "It's like yelling fire in a very, very crowded theater," he said bitterly.

At the beginning of 2008, shares were down more than 83 percent, and Countrywide had been forced to draw on its entire credit line of $11.5 billion in order to stay afloat. On January 11, 2008, Bank of America swept in with a surprise announcement that it would purchase Countrywide for $4.1 billion in stock, a rock-bottom price at only $7.16 a share. I asked Bank of America CEO Ken Lewis why he would buy such a troubled business since many analysts believed things would only get worse. Lewis was a measured guy, not the least bit flamboyant. Risk taking wasn't his thing but deal making was. Steadily and quietly, he'd built Bank of America through a string of acquisitions, including Fleet and MBNA. Now his sights were on Countrywide. From Lewis's perspective, Bank of America wanted a deal, and it got a deal. He figured that a year earlier his company would have forked over around $26 a share for Countrywide. So he was comfortable that Bank of America had done due diligence—more, he told me, than had ever been done before with other deals. And he stressed that Bank of America was not getting into subprime. There would be no more subprime business from Countrywide.

And what of Angelo Mozilo? Here Ken Lewis displayed a thin pretense of warmth. "I know there have been criticisms of Angelo," he said, "but beneath the surface there is a wonderful human being. I think he's gotten a bad rap at times."

"But he won't be staying with the company, right?" I asked.

"Right," Lewis said. "He's sixty-nine years old. He would like to see this through and spend more time with his grandchildren."

But the picture of Angelo Mozilo, serenely retired with grandchildren perched on his knees, was not to be. On June 4, 2009, the SEC, in a civil suit, charged Mozilo, David Sambol, and former chief financial officer Eric Sieracki with securities fraud; Mozilo was also charged with insider trading, but as of this writing the court cases have failed to materialize.

Countrywide wasn't the only early victim of subprime lending. Companies such as New Century Financial Corporation and American Home Mortgage Investment Corporation, leading subprime lenders, filed Chapter 11, with more bankruptcies anticipated. If the fallout had been limited to the lenders themselves it might have been contained. But by the time Countrywide was acquired by Bank of America, the worthless mortgage securities bundles were embedded in the system, pulling down some of the giants of investment banking from the United States to Europe and Asia.

The story of the financial industry's collapse is still being written, but looking back we can pinpoint the warning signs. Nobody was paying attention to the interconnectedness of all the industries. Problems in the housing market were viewed as severe, but people were talking about it as if it were just the health of one industry that was at stake. Not true. The housing market was linked to the investment banks and ultimately to the newly globalized financial system, and when the thread was pulled, everything began to unravel.

Even those in the top echelon of the nation's economy failed to recognize the looming crisis presented by subprime. Before he stepped down as Fed chairman, Alan Greenspan disputed suggestions of a housing bubble, calling it nothing more than "froth" in certain markets. Ben Bernanke, then chairman of the president's Council of Economic Advisers and soon to replace Greenspan, told Congress that he believed the boom reflected positive aspects in the economy, like job and housing growth. Neither Greenspan nor Bernanke expressed any real concern that a housing bubble might be growing that could place the economy in peril if it burst.

To be fair, not everyone was swept up in the subprime craze. A small but potent movement was emerging, composed of traders who had no confidence in subprime assets. Leading the charge was John Paulson, a former managing director of Bear Stearns, who in 2006 set up his company, Paulson Credit Opportunities Fund, for the sole purpose of shorting subprime mortgage-backed assets. Paulson was an early predictor that the subprime market would crash. With his colleague, Paolo Pellegrini, he made $2.7 billion in 2007, betting against subprime.

Short selling involves borrowing stock (usually from a brokerage), selling, and then waiting for the price to drop. When (and if) it does, you buy it back at the lower price, replace the stock, and pocket the difference. Short-sellers are rarely looked upon fondly by corporate America—and why would they be? Short-sellers essentially bet against the system. They predict failure, and they earn profits when stocks sink.

A colleague of mine once compared short selling to Pete Rose betting against baseball. Some people believe it is unethical. Short-sellers like Paulson and Pellegrini would argue that they actually perform a valuable service by injecting an honest evaluation of worth into the process. My own view is that there is nothing wrong with short selling. This is what makes a market: a buyer and a seller. Short-sellers do not create a crisis in confidence. It is ludicrous to blame short-sellers, unless they are behaving fraudulently. And I have often seen short-sellers do much more research than "long" analysts. Short selling is just one more strategy, so long as the investor is not spreading false information and creating a run on institutions, the way some Wall Street executives charged during the 2008 period.

Is there a larger obligation—even a patriotic duty—to protect the markets? I have heard people say that short-sellers are abdicating a core responsibility of citizenship. Short-sellers hate being called peddlers of the system's destruction. In our system, some companies do well and others don't. You're allowed to point out the companies you think are on the wrong track, and bet against them.

"You can't put much blame on short selling for bringing companies down," a source at the Treasury once told me. "Most of the time when the company fails it's because the company is inherently a bad company. The short-sellers just saw it early."

I was interested, though, in what Paulson and Pellegrini saw that others didn't. In 2010 I asked Pellegrini to describe the reasons for their decision to buck the trend and bet against subprime. He told me that it was not a grand scheme.

"We were only looking for investment opportunities with a lot of upside and little downside," he said. "And when we first looked at subprime, we made a general observation that there was generally too much leverage in the economy—and, in particular, there was too much leverage with housing.

"We were all familiar with the different mortgages that were being offered, including those we had been exposed to personally, and the subprime just didn't make any sense. We started investigating that, and since it was so inexpensive to bet against those mortgages, we started doing that, too, in a fairly conservative way. It took time for us to understand all of the intricacies and solve some of the puzzles. For example, why didn't these mortgages go bad faster? What was propping them up? Asking those questions led us to investigate the housing practices of the lenders with respect to pricing, appraisals, refinancing, and the whole operating philosophy. How could they expect to keep borrowers current despite the fact that the borrowers really didn't have the wherewithal to pay the mortgages?" It was, I realized, the question too few people were asking—at least not publicly.

It turns out there were plenty of worried faces at the Treasury as early as the summer of 2007. Hank Paulson viewed the freeze of the credit markets with growing alarm. Sure, the stock market was booming, but he could see the underlying paralysis beginning to form. "No one voiced it publicly," a former Treasury official told me. "But behind the scenes we were thinking that any moment Armageddon was going to happen."

―――――

Bear Stearns, the eighty-five-year-old investment bank, was considered something of a cowboy firm, and that reputation was personified by its seventy-four-year-old, swashbuckling, cigar-chomping leader, Jimmy Cayne. That Cayne was the face of Bear Stearns was galling to some, who found him an indifferent administrator and personally embarrassing. The rap on Cayne was that, in his later years, he preferred playing golf and bridge to running Bear, although some of his executives defended him as being unconventional yet brilliant.

The most destructive legacy of Cayne's reign would be the way he allowed individuals at Bear to construct their own unsupervised fiefdoms. One of these was Ralph Cioffi, who ran a fund backed by home mortgages. In 2007, as the mortgage market tanked, Cioffi found himself stuck with billions of dollars of mortgage-backed securities that nobody would buy. What to do? Cioffi came up with a scheme to repackage them, using a new public company called Everquest Financial. Through his new company, Cioffi hoped to unload his bad securities.

But the scheme was outed by the business press, and Bear Stearns was forced to withdraw the offering. It would later mean a federal indictment for Cioffi, but he was ultimately acquitted of all charges. However, the chief effect of the failed offering was to turn a floodlight on Bear's problems—in particular, weak, inattentive leadership.

One person growing disillusioned with Cayne's performance was Bear's eighty-one-year-old chairman, Alan "Ace" Greenberg. A Bear lifer who started as a clerk in 1949 and was CEO from 1978 to 1993, Greenberg was notorious as an administrative tightwad, recycling paper clips and rubber bands to hold expenses down. He had a reputation for being a man of integrity—an example being his dictate that company officers give 4 percent of their gross salary to charity. In many respects, Greenberg was an old-fashioned banker who didn't appreciate the fast-and-loose climate of Cayne's regime. He and Cayne had always been very close, but now their relationship was feeling the strain. In 2010 Greenberg would write a book, *The Rise and Fall of Bear Stearns*, detailing his many grievances against Cayne. Among them was Cayne's unabashed striving for prestige. "In Jimmy's case, that hunger for money and status, and the gamesmanship that went with it, indicated an insecurity that was no blessing at all," he wrote.

When I asked Greenberg what went wrong, he seemed pained by his falling out with Cayne, although the end was inevitable in light of Cayne's behavior. "His relationship with me certainly changed over the years," Greenberg told me. "If I said something was white, he said it was black."

On November 1, 2007, the *Wall Street Journal* published a scathing critique of Cayne, portraying him as a modern-day Nero, playing bridge while Bear Stearns burned. In particular, the article cited Cayne's absence during the summer meltdown of two of Bear's hedge funds. He was at a bridge tournament in Tennessee where there was no cell phone or e-mail access. The article also mentioned reports that Cayne smoked pot in his Bear Stearns office, which, combined with everything else, made him look sloppy and irresponsible.

With Bear's stock falling, the article could not have come at a worse time for Cayne. After the company announced in December that it would write down $1.9 billion in mortgage-related securities and suffer the first quarterly loss in its history, the board demanded Cayne's resignation. He agreed to go quietly. He was replaced by Bear president Alan Schwartz, a Brooklyn-born financier who had been with the company for thirty-two years. Schwartz was a Cayne loyalist, but he couldn't have been more different. He was a skilled and experienced manager, and given a bit more time, he might have pulled Bear out of the hole. But Schwartz didn't realize when he took over as CEO that the firm had just about run out of time. Throughout January and February things only grew worse as Bear was assaulted by a constant drumbeat in the media about its problems. Schwartz was outraged by the reports—especially those made by Charlie Gasparino, then a reporter for CNBC. Gasparino was amping up the rhetoric to a fever pitch, saying that Bear Stearns was worried about a run on the bank, not by short-sellers but by its prime customers. Schwartz fought back as best he could. He claimed that Bear's problems were being wildly overstated, as part of a media-fueled feeding frenzy. Bear Stearns, he insisted, was solid.

On Wednesday, March 12, 2008, the headlines were focused on the shocking downfall of New York governor Eliot Spitzer, who resigned that day in the wake of revelations that he'd regularly had sex with prostitutes. It was a big story for those of us in the business media. When he was attorney general, Spitzer had been the self-appointed avenging angel of Wall Street who seemed to relish the perp walk for high-profile financiers—even though he didn't always have the goods on them before he brought them down. There was no small glee on Wall Street at Spitzer's fall into the tabloid muck in light of the purity tests he imposed upon the financial community, although some people had a classier response. "I don't get any joy out of anyone's pain," Larry Fink of BlackRock told me, adding that "the market always gets overjoyed with other people's pain, whether it's other firms losing money or other executives falling down." He didn't share the excitement, calling it nothing more than an ugly moment in New York.

A secondary story we had been tracking all week also involved pain on many levels—pain for employees and stockholders of the venerable Bear Stearns. Rumors had been intensifying that Bear was running out of cash, and those rumors had a paralyzing effect on cash flow to the struggling investment bank.

On that Wednesday, Schwartz reluctantly appeared on CNBC to try to stop the rumors. He insisted once again that Bear was healthy and claimed not to know where the rumors originated. "Part of the problem is that when speculation starts in a market that has a lot of emotion in it, and people are concerned about the volatility, then people will sell first and ask questions later, and that creates its own momentum," he said plaintively.

His point was well taken, but was it accurate to say that Bear Stearns was merely a victim of the rumor mill? Granted, the financial press has a key role to play and must play it responsibly to prevent overreaction or false reactions in the market. But there seemed to be a lot of rot under the surface at Bear, and it was disingenuous to blame the media. Watching Schwartz, I thought, "Don't shoot the messenger. What's the real truth?" False optimism is never warranted, and the consequences are very real. A source of mine complained quite angrily about Schwartz. After watching him give assurances on CNBC, my source bought shares in Bear Stearns and ended up losing a million dollars.

Today, looking back on Schwartz's claims of solvency during a period when clearly Bear was about to fail, I want to give him the benefit of the doubt. At the time, Bear had a strong balance sheet, so Schwartz's claim was essentially true. What he didn't measure was the destructive effect of a run on the bank. It was a slippery slope. The markets move fast, and at the hint of trouble, a run on Bear could demolish it.

———

Jamie Dimon was a youthful fifty-two—shrewd but personable, with one of the best résumés on the Street. He was born on Long Island of Greek heritage, a twin who was also the son and grandson of stockbrokers, and he chose to follow in their footsteps while forging his own identity. As a young man he was irreverent, long-haired, and bright, and he retained his shaggy style through Harvard Business School.

More than anything, what may have determined Dimon's future was his choice of a mentor—a friend of the family named Sandy Weill, who had just become president of American Express. Weill had made a name for himself as brilliant but iconoclastic, and he was happy to take Dimon under his wing. After graduating from Harvard, Dimon accepted a job with Weill, as his assistant at Amex.

As Weill's protégé, Dimon was whip smart and deeply loyal. The two men were like father and son, and Dimon was so attached to his mentor that when Weill resigned from Amex in 1985 because the firm wouldn't make him chairman, Dimon followed him out the door. They experienced some lean years together, but by 1998 they had come back with a vengeance, building the empire that would become Citigroup. By then their bond was so tight that everyone expected Dimon to be Weill's successor when he eventually retired. But that didn't come to pass.

If Weill had an Achilles' heel, some people felt it was his outsize ego. He enjoyed being the headmaster, the man in the spotlight. Citigroup's name was synonymous with Weill, and he wanted to keep it that way. As long as Jamie Dimon stayed in his place as the obedient, subservient son and heir-in-waiting, Weill was pleased with him. But when Dimon began establishing his own reputation and getting noticed by the press, Weill became touchy about not being the total center of attention. Although Dimon was hardly a media hound, the press warmed to the young, handsome financier, and he couldn't always control it. As a result, the relationship between the two men began to fray. Then Dimon did the unthinkable—at least from Weill's standpoint. He disrespected a member of the family.

Weill's daughter, Jessica Bibliowicz, had joined the firm, and by all accounts Dimon welcomed her. But then Weill asked Dimon to put her in charge of Smith Barney, a unit of Citi. Dimon demurred, politely but firmly telling Weill that she was not ready to take on such a big responsibility. When Weill's daughter resigned rather than accept a lesser position, Dimon's goose was cooked. Weill could never look at him the same way again. He'd betrayed the king. Off with his head. In 1998 Weill fired Dimon.

Later Weill wrote a book, which he told me was a cathartic effort to get over the pain of the separation. "Jamie was incredibly smart and unbelievably loyal," he said sadly. "He was a terrific partner who I really loved, and I hated to see our relationship come to an end. Unfortunately, it had to."

Weill's version implied that the split was Dimon's doing, and with a guy like Weill, there could be no convincing him otherwise. Dimon wasn't talking. He may have been deeply wounded by Weill's actions, but he kept his feelings to himself. Eventually he bounced back, becoming the CEO of Bank One, which he then sold to JPMorgan Chase for $58 billion—a deal widely praised as good for everyone. In 2004 Dimon became the president and chief operating officer of JPMorgan and was made CEO the following year. He was admired on Wall Street and in Washington, and his recent claim to fame was that he'd limited JPMorgan's exposure to subprime. He was also beloved by his people. One of his lieutenants told me, "Jamie inspires confidence," and his team was extremely loyal to him.

On the evening of Dimon's fifty-second birthday, Thursday, March 13, he received a desperate call on his cell phone from Alan Schwartz. JPMorgan was the clearing bank for Bear Stearns, and Schwartz put it to him straight: he needed $30 billion, and he needed it *now*. Dimon was shaken by the immediacy of the request, and he told Schwartz it was impossible—at least not without some kind of federal guarantee. He suggested that Schwartz put in a call to Timothy Geithner at the Federal Reserve.

Geithner took the call from Schwartz and sprang into action. Schwartz had warned him that bankruptcy was imminent without a rescue, and he was grim as he began to work the phones. He real-

ized how damaging it was to be caught so off guard. Only days earlier Christopher Cox, chairman of the SEC, had told reporters, "We
have a good deal of comfort about the capital cushions" at Bear.
What the hell had happened?

Geithner's concern went far beyond the fate of a single investment bank. He believed Bear's struggle was a gateway to a systemic
crisis that could have a devastating impact on U.S. and global markets. He likened it to a spreading contagion, whose origins were
small but whose rapid, multiplying effect could bring down the financial infrastructure.

"The news that Bear's liquidity position was so dire that a bankruptcy filing was imminent presented us with a very difficult set of policy judgments," he would explain to a congressional committee months
later. "In our financial system, the market sorts out which companies
survive and which fail. However, under the circumstances prevailing in
the markets the issues raised in this specific instance extended well beyond the fate of one company. It became clear that Bear's involvement
in the complex and intricate web of relationships that characterize our
financial system, at a point in time when markets were especially vulnerable, was such that a sudden failure would likely lead to a chaotic
unwinding of positions in already damaged markets. Moreover, a failure by Bear to meet its obligations would have cast a cloud of doubt on
the financial position of other institutions whose business models bore
some superficial similarity to Bear's, without due regard for the fundamental soundness of those firms."

Whether or not Geithner's analysis was accurate, there is no
question that his response to the crisis was forceful and immediate.
On the Thursday that Schwartz sounded the alarm, he assembled
teams in New York and Washington, D.C., that worked overnight to

study the situation and come up with potential solutions. A group of examiners was dispatched from the New York Fed to examine Bear's books. Geithner also held conversations with Dimon, who reiterated his contention that JPMorgan was a potential purchaser but would require a federal backstop. Dimon was not willing to take a big risk. His primary obligation was to his own shareholders. He also knew far more than other banks as he was the lender to some of those vulnerable institutions.

As dawn broke over lower Manhattan Friday morning, Geithner held another conference call with the Fed board of governors and members of the Treasury Department to review the options and decide on a way forward. They settled on a stopgap measure to buy some time. With the support of Treasury secretary Paulson, Fed chairman Bernanke, and the board of governors, it was agreed that the New York Fed would help engineer a rescue.

The arrangement that was presented to Schwartz on Friday morning was nothing short of a lifeline. JPMorgan Chase would issue a credit line, backed by the Fed, good for twenty-eight days. Schwartz, who had never accepted that his company was on the brink of ruin, believed he could secure capital or engineer a lucrative sale in that period of time. But that's when things got weird. Late Friday, Geithner told Schwartz he didn't have twenty-eight days, after all. The federal money would be available only for the weekend. Schwartz was stunned. He felt betrayed, although he subsequently shrugged it off as a misunderstanding on his part: he thought they'd said twenty-eight days; they'd actually said two.

To this day it isn't entirely clear what happened. It seems unlikely that Schwartz was confused. With his company in dire jeopardy, would he make such an error? More plausible is the explanation that as they studied Bear's books, the Feds decided the risk was too great. The cord had to be cut by Sunday night.

Overnight deals are the most stressful kind, especially when the stakes are so high. While several firms initially expressed interest in Bear Stearns, it was nearly impossible to perform the due diligence, create a plan, and get the approvals in the space of forty-eight hours. The question was, who had the nerve, the independence, and the cash to make it work? The answer kept returning to JPMorgan Chase. By late Saturday it was the only buyer left. But the deal was constantly threatened by the hard realities Dimon's people faced as they scoured Bear's books.

"It happened very quickly," a source at the White House who was monitoring the situation told me. "In the days before their fateful weekend, they were trading at around $40 a share. Bear Stearns looked like a solvent company even as of Friday morning before it failed. We had these issues that we thought were liquidity issues, where the institutions simply couldn't raise the money to cover their short-term obligations, but they were solvent in the sense that the value of their assets exceeded the value of their liabilities. The problem was that they became illiquid and they couldn't raise the money, so they had to start dumping assets. And the assets no longer were worth as much as they thought they were. The liquidity crisis turned into a solvency crisis, and it happened, literally, within hours."

When I spoke with Dimon the following month, he shook his head in amazement, recalling the weekend. "It's the last time I will ever do something like that," he said. "You have to know that there were two hundred people from JPMorgan and probably an equal number of people from Bear Stearns working around the clock.

They didn't go to sleep for a two- or three-day period. Just watching that teamwork of those folks was something special. But it was brutal. It's unprecedented in a forty-eight-hour period that two companies and the government get together and pull off a transaction like that."

The most brutal aspect of the negotiations was setting the price. "It was really hard to come up with a price," Dimon acknowledged. "The question was, how much risk could JPMorgan bear? We wanted to make sure that JPMorgan was never put in a position where it was jeopardized in any way, shape, or form."

What Dimon didn't mention was that, behind the scenes, Paulson was pushing for a lower price, not wanting the appearance that the government was rewarding a failing company for its misdeeds. The concept he invoked was that of "moral hazard"; that is, if the government was seen as rescuing a company whose bad choices were responsible for its failures, other companies would not be discouraged from making similar bad choices. Paulson was also extremely sensitive to the fact that Bear's rescue would be achieved with the backing of taxpayer money, and he was loath to abuse the privilege. Throughout the weekend the discussions about the bid seemed to range from $8 to $12 a share. But as time began to run out, the number started to shrink precipitously.

I was working at home when I got the call that Bear Stearns was being sold to JPMorgan for $2 a share. I couldn't believe it. Perhaps my source had dropped a zero?

It's hard to fully describe the consequences of such a low share price. To put it in context, a year earlier Bear was trading at around $170 a share. To no one's surprise, shareholder rage in the wake of the announcement was intense. Amid charges of highway robbery,

Dimon was forced to go back to the table and push the share price to $10. However, Dimon would later defend the rock-bottom original price to Congress with the explanation, "Buying a house is not the same as buying a house on fire."

Ace Greenberg would later describe to me how heartsick he felt on that day. "My regret was that we had fourteen thousand marvelous people working for us that were so loyal, and many had been there so long. We had people who were challenged as runners and so forth, and they wouldn't miss a day of work. Snow, subway strike, these people, believe me, were there every day. It was just marvelous. And I felt very bad. I was afraid they weren't going to get jobs."

Still, the sale was widely believed to be a success. A Treasury Department insider who was involved with the deal told me, "The reason Bear Stearns is important is because we could never have pulled off something so major in a weekend without everyone—the Fed, the Treasury, the banks—understanding how disastrous failure would be. Everyone knew the situation was dire—that we *had* to come up with a deal."

With the sale in place, Paulson breathed a sigh of relief. They'd dodged a major bullet. One of his advisers said, "Well, you've had your big moment, Mr. Secretary. Bear Stearns will be what you're remembered for."

If only that were true.

THREE

Zombies at Lehman

"The investment banking model is a confidence game; it's about funding. There's no one in the world who could have raised money for Goldman, Morgan Stanley, Lehman, Merrill. Forget it. Everyone was like, 'I'm staying out of this thing.'"
—A FORMER LEHMAN BROTHERS EXECUTIVE

SEPTEMBER 12, 2008

At the Federal Reserve, the CEO working groups labored on, late into the evening, trying to get a handle on the true condition of Lehman Brothers. The mood was tense and at times sorrowful. Later, I received a call from one of the men that was quite telling. "Paulson made it very clear that there would be no Fed bailout," he said. "It's up to us." He sounded drained as he described sitting at a table at the New York Fed along with Geithner, Paulson, and the Lehman people. He said, "Across the table the Lehman guys truly looked like zombies. And it was at that moment that we all realized, 'Oh my God, these guys could go bankrupt. They could actually file, and if they do, it's going to impact all of us.'"

Meanwhile, Fuld and his team were closeted in Lehman's midtown offices. As rain pelted the thirty-first-floor windows, they worked furiously to find a way to structure a deal that would be acceptable to a potential buyer. That meant packaging and unloading the toxic assets.

Paulson called Fuld Friday evening. "I told the group that they should think about a consortium to buy Lehman Brothers, and they turned it down," he told him.

Fuld was disappointed but he kept pushing. "We need another idea," he told his team, and one of the men in the room said, "Okay, I have a different idea. Why don't you just get them to guarantee the debt on the commercial real estate. That's the thing people are pointing the finger at. That's why they're asking, 'Is there a hole in the balance sheet?' We put in $10 billion of equity, and the debt's guaranteed by the consortium—say another $30 billion. Checkmate. Done."

Fuld called Paulson back and floated the idea.

"Great. I'll bring it into the room," Paulson said.

He called back within a half hour. "No, they don't want to do that."

"It was frustrating," Scott Friedheim, the chief administrative officer and one of Fuld's closest allies and advisers, recalled later. "We'd come up with idea after idea, and every single one of them got shot down." He felt exhausted and demoralized.

———

Scott Friedheim was a young man, only forty-two, but his body was screaming at him, "Slow down, slow down." That was the one thing he could not do. In the months leading up to September 12, he had been putting in seven-day weeks, and very long days. Later he would tell me with a wry laugh, "When I heard people saying they didn't sleep for a week during the peak of the crisis, I thought, 'Oh my God, for us it's been since March.' We were in full-battle mode all quarter long. We were in there every frickin' weekend."

In early August, on a rare Sunday afternoon away from the office, Friedheim was visiting a colleague at home. "He had a small basketball hoop for his kids, and I went to dunk it in the short basket," he recalled. "I didn't even get off the ground. I just planted my leg and a tendon popped out of my hip, broke the hip and tore the labrum, and I went down. I had to be in the office the next day, and I was there, popping Tylenol and in tremendous pain. My doctor said, 'Stay in bed, rest, keep off the hip for three months.' Yeah, right."

To further complicate matters, he was getting married in the South of France over Labor Day weekend. He almost didn't make it.

Two weeks before the wedding, while Friedheim was still hobbling on crutches, Dick Fuld came into his office. A five-ten former weight lifter, Fuld was an intense guy, and now he directed the full force of that intensity on Friedheim, saying, "I've got good news and bad news."

Friedheim didn't crack a smile. "Give me the bad news," he said with a sense of doom.

"You can't go," Fuld said.

"To my wedding?"

"Right."

Friedheim was so flabbergasted that all he could think of to say was, "And the good news?"

Fuld gave him an intense look. "The good news is I need you."

Friedheim felt a momentary surge of exhausted resentment. He hadn't had a full day off in a year, and now this. He started explaining to Fuld the magnitude of the wedding event. "I have four hundred people coming to the South of France, and most of the families are already there at the château we rented," he said, "and you expect me to just say I'm not coming?" He didn't bother stating the obvious, that it wasn't just the inconvenience of it—it was his *wedding day*, arguably one of life's most significant moments, and his boss was telling him to choose the company over his fiancée and his personal future. If he hadn't known Fuld better, he would have called the suggestion that he miss his own wedding stone-cold preposterous. But Fuld wasn't cold. He was just focused—a surgeon with his arm already elbow deep in his patient's chest cavity. Lehman was on life support and there was no time for niceties.

That Friedheim didn't go ballistic was a credit to the loyalty Fuld inspired. In spite of his lack of personal charisma, Fuld evoked something akin to a cultlike fervor among his staff. Lehman Brothers was like a religion to them, worthy of any sacrifice. It was also like a family, growing more close knit in the face of crisis. When Fuld challenged his workers to "bleed Lehman green," they were proud to comply, if not literally, then emotionally.

Friedheim did some quick calculating, trying to figure out how he could meet Fuld's demand and still show up for his wedding. He canceled his flight and booked a red-eye that would put him on site hours before the ceremony. He made it, but he was so dead tired that after one dance with his new wife, Isabelle, he said, "I'm sorry. I've got to go to sleep. I'm exhausted."

He slept for a few hours and took the earliest flight back to New

York, still negotiating on crutches. Not exactly a romantic weekend. "It was absolutely brutal," he recalled, and yet in a funny way it seemed completely justified. He'd been with Lehman for eighteen years, loyal and dedicated. Lehman was his first wife, and Friedheim was desperately trying to save his marriage. And although that meant getting off to a precarious start in his marriage to Isabelle, he didn't hesitate.

———

The urgency had been building ever since Bear's fire sale to JPMorgan. As much as everybody would have hoped that Bear Stearns was the finale of the crisis rather than the beginning, it was immediately evident that it was a harbinger of worse things to come. The investment banking model was being called into question. From the outset, the Fed was concerned about Lehman. Its similarities to Bear Stearns were inescapable—in particular, poor liquidity and too many real estate assets. Indeed, rumors that Lehman would be the next investment bank to fall sent its shares plunging by nearly 50 percent the Monday after Bear's sale. Bank executives would later tell me that the assets owned by Lehman were significantly riskier than Bear's or any other firm's.

Thursday, March 20, 2008, I interviewed Lehman's CFO, Erin Callan, on *Closing Bell*. Callan was an anomaly on Wall Street—a young, forty-two-year-old woman in the top echelon of a legendary firm. She was smart, pretty, and media savvy, and although she had not been in her position long, she had increasingly become Lehman's public face and primary cheerleader. Some people suggested that Dick Fuld, who hated appearing in the media, sent her out so he didn't have to go. Fuld was always awkward around the press. He never really knew how to be the face of Lehman, and he wasn't interested in playing the role. He despised the snarky attitudes and personal slights—such as the way he was dubbed "the gorilla" in the press. He spoke to reporters only on background.

Callan was not universally popular inside Lehman. Sources told me they worried that Fuld pushed her out front too much, and not always to positive effect. She was unquestionably bright and ambitious—a Long Island girl who rose to become the first female member of Lehman Brothers' executive committee. She was mentored by Lehman president Joe Gregory, and he thought the world of her. But others in the organization wondered whether a former tax lawyer had the proper grounding in financial services. In fact, she was among the bankers working on several high-profile financial service IPOs before being elevated to CFO.

Many people at Lehman were also dismayed by Callan's flashy public persona. A glowing profile in the March 2008 issue of *Condé Nast Portfolio* was titled "Wall Street's Most Powerful Woman" and pictured Callan emerging from a limo showing a lot of leg. The article by Sheelah Kolhatkar emphasized Callan's femininity, describing her "short crocheted dress with a black belt slung low around her hips, gold hoop earrings, and knee-high caramel-colored high-heel boots." Callan didn't mind the focus. "I don't subordinate my feminine side," she told Kolhatkar. "I'm very open about it. I have no problem talking about my [personal] shopper or my outfit."

Then a May 2008 *Wall Street Journal* profile of Callan raised eyebrows further and annoyed many people with its centerpiece photo of Callan, looking slinky in an above-the-knee black dress and very high stiletto heels. "She seems to be everywhere modeling her wardrobe," one insider complained to me. "I wouldn't mind, but does she know what she's doing?"

As a woman in the men's club of finance, I had some sympathy for Callan. Women always faced this kind of scrutiny, and it wasn't entirely fair. I was more interested in the substance of Callan's position and contribution.

Callan was an extremely smart woman, and I always found her very knowledgeable. But there was no question that she was on the defensive after Bear went down.

"Is Lehman next?" I asked her.

"Categorically no," she said without hesitation. "It's really rumor. I mean, every time the markets are under pressure, Lehman is supposedly hanging on by its fingernails. We fully anticipated that Monday was going to be a very, very difficult day for us, that we would be a top target, and we had a game plan to address it. But how do you get yourself out of that predicament? It just takes time and patience, proving ourselves in a tough environment."

I pushed back. "I have a hard time understanding how things could change so fast and furiously for Bear. Can your business really reverse course like that in a forty-eight-hour period, or was that perhaps a situation unique to Bear?"

"I think that will be the lingering question about our industry and our business model," she said carefully, while insisting that Lehman was sound. Callan didn't want people to start thinking about dominoes falling.

Callan returned to my show on April 1 to respond to reports that Lehman was looking to raise additional capital. "Good to see you a little sooner than expected," she said, making a sour face. "Unfortunately, we're in a market where perception trumps reality." She went on to make the case that Lehman's efforts in no way showed desperation.

One person who was not impressed with Callan's explanations was David Einhorn, the young president of Greenlight Capital, who had become a thorn in Lehman's side. In April he reported that he was shorting Lehman stock, and he started doing frequent television interviews deriding Lehman. Callan was upset. She felt that Einhorn didn't fully understand Lehman's position. When Einhorn asked for a conference call, Callan was wary, fearing a setup. But Fuld wanted her to do it, so she went ahead. The call was a disaster. Einhorn publicly disputed her claims and said that he wasn't impressed by her poorly prepared answers to his questions.

Einhorn made no secret of his belief that Callan was woefully unqualified—and worse, that she was presenting phony numbers, inflating assets, and burying problems. On May 21, Einhorn made a speech at the prestigious Ira W. Sohn Investment Research Conference, which coincided with the publication of his book, *Fooling Some of the People All of the Time.*

In his speech, which was by turns fiery and sarcastic, Einhorn pointed out that some entities had made investments that they believed would generate smooth returns, but the investments couldn't deliver. "The decline in current market values has forced these institutions to make a tough decision," he said. "Do they follow the rules, take the write-downs, and suffer the consequences whatever they may be? Or worse, do they take the view that they can't really value the investments in order to avoid writing them down? Or, even worse, do they claim to follow the accounting rules, but simply lie about the values? The turn of the cycle has created some tough choices. Warren Buffett has said, 'You don't know who is swimming naked until the tide goes out.'" And clearly, Einhorn believed, the tide had gone out on Lehman Brothers and exposed plenty. He directed particularly scathing criticism toward Callan. Citing their conference call about quarter two results, he jabbed at her, noting, "Erin Callan used the word 'great' fourteen times, 'challenging' six times, 'strong' twenty-four times, and 'tough' once. She used the word 'incredibly' eight times. I would use 'incredible' in a different way to describe the report."

But then he went in for the kill. "For the last several weeks, Lehman has been complaining about short-sellers," he said. "Academic research and our experience indicate that when management teams do that, it is a sign that management is attempting to distract investors from serious problems. I think that there is enough evidence to show how Lehman answered the difficult question as to whether to tell the truth and suffer the consequences or not. This raises the question, though, of what incentive do corporate managers have to fully acknowledge bad news in a truthful fashion?

"For the capital markets to function," he concluded, "companies need to provide investors with accurate information rather than whatever numbers add up to a smooth return. If there is no penalty for misbehavior—and, in fact, such behavior is rewarded with flattering stories in the mainstream press about how to handle a crisis—we will all bear the negative consequences over time."

Callan was livid—not just because Einhorn was shorting Lehman's stock, but because he was attacking her so publicly. In an interview with me, she called on the SEC to investigate the predatory tactics of short-sellers like Einhorn. Fuld was also angry. He vowed to "hurt" the shorts.

I wondered how valid Einhorn's perspective was. I asked Brad

Hintz, who had been Lehman's CFO in the 1990s, putting it to him this way: "Einhorn is basically claiming that what Lehman said in the first quarter is not what it's saying now with regard to its portfolio. He's all but said Lehman is deceiving investors. Do you think Dick Fuld and Erin Callan have been as forthright as they might have been?"

"If you're asking me whether Lehman will win an award for best disclosure, the answer is no," Hintz replied. "But I don't think any brokerage firm will get that. Are there numbers gaps? Absolutely. I don't doubt that. But I think the concerns from the shorts are overdone." Hintz didn't believe the risk to Lehman was that severe. "Lehman will not go down. We have the Federal Reserve behind it. By the Fed opening the discount window, it has injected a little bit of courage into the counterparties. So when Lehman says, 'We're not borrowing much from the Fed,' that's technically very true. But they are borrowing courage." Ultimately, Einhorn proved to be right.

As Lehman and other companies struggled, the people trying to hold them together were working overtime, exploring multiple options. It was complex and it was tricky. Fuld was frequently on the phone with the Treasury Department, discussing options. Paulson would later say that they spoke some fifty times between April and September. Paulson was often frustrated with Fuld, who he believed had trouble seeing and accepting reality.

As one of Paulson's cohorts told me, "It really became apparent over the summer that no one had the same view as Dick of what Lehman was worth. Now, I think Dick is a fine guy, but he just wouldn't wake up and smell the coffee. We at the Treasury began to focus on Lehman Brothers immediately after Bear Stearns went down. We were in frequent touch with Dick. Actually, Dick was in India the weekend that Bear Stearns went down. And I talked to him two or three times in India that weekend and said, 'You've got to get back. There's going to be a laserlike focus on Lehman.' But there were serious doubts about whether Fuld was getting the message."

If Fuld's expectations seemed unreasonably high, it may have been because of his past experience. Ten years earlier, Fuld had been the hero who rescued Lehman when the collapse of the hedge fund Long-Term Capital almost brought the firm down. He believed he could pull off another rescue.

In the early summer Lehman was in discussions with several potential strategic international partners. Fuld had long been interested in developing a collaboration with a foreign company, with the partner taking a 5 to 7 percent stake in Lehman.

"Every weekend we were at the office, busted up into teams, discussing options," a former Lehman executive told me. "We thought we could do any number of things. For example, if for the third quarter, instead of announcing the numbers we did, we'd reported having sold $10 billion of the risky mortgages and now had no mortgages on the books; or if we had announced a spin-off with $10 billion in equity, and the debt on the books was guaranteed by JPMorgan; or if we'd sold the investment management division for $6 billion and made a profit, and our leverage was strong and we'd be good to go. Or if we'd announced that we got a $10 billion investment from Korea Development Bank, or we'd sold the company to Bank of America, everyone would be applauding us. These were all valid options under consideration."

Then something inexplicable and shattering occurred that put a huge dent in Lehman's credibility. On Wednesday, June 4, a story appeared in the *Wall Street Journal*, "Lehman Is Seeking Overseas Capital: As Its Stock Declines, Wall Street Firm Expands Search For Cash, May Tap Korea." The story highlighting Lehman's liquidity problems was written by business reporter Sue Craig, and it cited a source high up in the executive office. This was potentially devastating for the company because it proved Lehman needed cash. Who would talk to the *Journal*, especially to reveal such a strategy? That day Lehman's stock dropped like a stone, leaving the top executives baffled and horrified.

Scott Friedheim had a vague suspicion of who might have been Craig's source. That morning, Erin Callan came into his office and sat down. It was the first time she'd ever done that. Dick Fuld and Joe Gregory did it all the time. Callan never did. And she said, "What do you think of the *Journal* story? Do you think our stock is going to go up?"

Friedheim stared at her, bewildered. "No," he said, "I don't. I think it's going to go down." He couldn't believe she would see it that way, but her presence in his office raised his antennae. Why was she so eager to put a positive spin on it?

Dick Fuld was out for blood. What really got him was that he'd just spoken with Craig a week or two earlier. She'd called him and said, "I want to come in and sit in on one of your strategy sessions with your senior management team." She'd told Fuld that she was interested in getting an honest, and by implication, favorable picture of Lehman. Fuld said he couldn't let her sit in on actual strategy sessions, but he'd figure something out and get back to her. Then this happened. Feeling betrayed and blindsided, Fuld called Craig. "You posed as a friend of the firm," he said angrily, "and you're not what you said you were. You went behind my back, deceived me, and printed something that wasn't even true, and I'm not going to deal with you or the *Journal* again. We're through."

He slammed down the phone and turned to Friedheim. "Scott, no one in the firm talks to the *Journal*. That's it."

As Friedheim left Fuld's office, he continued to puzzle about the source of the story. Fuld had been so angry he hadn't thought to ask Craig. But as soon as he got back to his own office, Friedheim's phone rang. It was Kerrie Cohen, in public relations.

"Hey, Kerrie, what's up?" Friedheim said, distracted.

She said, "I just got the strangest call from Sue Craig." Friedheim sat up straight, now paying close attention.

"What did she say?"

"She was very angry," Cohen said. "She said, 'I just got off the phone with Dick. You have Erin call me immediately.' And then she hung up on me."

Now Friedheim felt it was likely that Callan was behind the *Journal* story. She'd apparently assured Craig that she was speaking with authority, and the reporter felt as if she'd been unfairly slammed by Fuld. Senior executives then checked the firm's e-mail records and said they found evidence that Callan had been talking to Craig.

I never had direct confirmation that Callan told Craig about the outreach to Korea and the possibility of a capital raise. But key people at the firm had their minds made up. It was the final self-inflicted wound Callan would sustain. In July she was forced out of Lehman.

I had Callan's cell phone number, so I called her when I heard the news. "Erin, it's Maria Bartiromo," I said when she answered. "I'm sorry about what has happened. Can you talk to me a little bit about what's going on?" She sighed and said, "Look, Maria, I've been crying all day. I'm sitting in the Hamptons having a glass of wine, and I'm done." Her voice trembled. "I can't stand them," she said.

"I want to keep in touch," she told me, and I agreed. We scheduled dinner for a month later, but she canceled a few days before the date. Although I had always been fair with her, I think Callan was in media-avoidance mode. No surprise there. Soon after, she joined Credit Suisse as managing director and head of the hedge fund business. She worked for only five months before taking an indefinite leave of absence and disappearing from public view. We didn't speak again.

———

The siege continued into 2008. "We had five months of total fear," Larry Fink, CEO of Blackrock, the largest asset manager, would confess to me later. He described a scenario that was nearly unprecedented, a dramatic loss of confidence in the markets. The conventional wisdom has always been that the markets are all-knowing—that there's an innate wisdom that never gets questioned. But suddenly, Fink explained, "the marketplace was frightened. Everything was very uncertain. The fear was quite large. I remember having dialogue with others—'Can we save all the companies? Should they all be saved?' Everyone wanted a positive resolution."

In fact, they were desperate for one. In interviews throughout the summer, I kept hearing shaky hope. The spin was nonstop. Everyone was using a baseball analogy to express some optimism. "We're in the eighth inning, Maria," they'd say. "We're in the bottom of the ninth." But when I spoke with Brad Hintz in June, he just laughed and called it a miscalculation. "A lot of the managements in these firms are saying, 'We're in the seventh inning . . . we're in the eighth inning.' The problem is, no one told them it was a doubleheader."

"It wasn't just Lehman on the line," an executive there told me. "Investment banking is a confidence game. If the market has zero confidence, every single one of us with this model is dead. It's not because we're bad firms."

The damage went beyond the banks, though. The growing mortgage crisis was also shaking the foundations of the large and sacrosanct Fannie Mae and Freddie Mac.

———

Dan Mudd, the head of Fannie Mae, found himself swept up in events during the summer of 2008. Mudd, fifty-two, the son of famed television newsman Roger Mudd, had been at Fannie Mae since 2000, and it had been a somewhat rocky tenure. A decorated Marine who served in Beirut, Mudd had established a solid business reputation internationally before he came to Fannie Mae, including serving as president of GE Capital Asia-Pacific and GE Capital-Japan. One day in early 2000, he received a call at his office in Tokyo from a headhunter, asking if he'd be interested in interviewing at Fannie Mae for the position of chief operating officer. Fannie Mae, an acronym for the Federal National Mortgage Association, was a government-sponsored company, chartered by Congress to provide liquidity, stability, and affordability to the housing market. Millions of Americans had mortgages through Fannie Mae and its counterpart, Freddie Mac (Federal Home Loan Mortgage Corporation). They were, in many people's eyes, the standard-bearers for the American dream.

Mudd said he wasn't interested in making a move, but the headhunter pressed him. "Why don't you at least talk to them, have breakfast or something the next time you're in Washington," he said. It turned out that Mudd was headed for Washington that week for his parents' fiftieth anniversary. He figured why not; he had nothing to lose. He arranged an interview with CEO Franklin Raines.

Raines, an accomplished businessman a few years older than Mudd, had an impressive résumé. He had been vice chairman of Fannie Mae for several years before joining the Clinton administration as the director of the Office of Management and Budget. He then returned to Fannie Mae as CEO once he'd left the administration. Raines's personal story was well known to Mudd. He was a classic example of someone who had pulled himself up by the bootstraps. The son of a Seattle janitor, he was the first African American to run a Fortune 500 company. But the initial meeting between Raines and Mudd did not go well.

"It was the worst interview of my life," Mudd later told me. "There was no chemistry, nothing there. The conversation didn't flow. It was like pulling teeth to get any answers from him." He left the interview shaking his head in disbelief. It had seemed like a colossal waste of time.

Mudd went back to Tokyo and forgot about it, but to his amazement, the headhunter called him a couple of weeks later and said, "Raines really liked you." He suggested that Mudd meet with board members and other principals.

The more Mudd thought about it, the more attractive the notion of moving back to Washington became. His parents and siblings lived there, and now that his children were approaching their teens, he thought it would be nice to be in the bosom of the extended family once again. He was also attracted to the job, to the idea of getting more involved in public policy, albeit in a market-oriented way. He believed he could make a contribution. He decided to take the plunge, and he started at the company in the winter of 2000.

It was a difficult adjustment. The pseudogovernmental nature of Fannie Mae was anathema to Mudd, who had always been a straight shooter in business. He had problems with the culture, the sense of secrecy, the constant need to double-check decisions for political implications. On a couple of occasions he almost resigned. Something seemed off about the agency, and off about Raines. In particular, Mudd found Raines's incessant lobbying and attempts to politicize his office distasteful.

In December 2004 he found out that his instincts were correct. He was sitting in his office when he received a call from Ann McLaughlin Korologos, the lead director. Korologos, the tough, no-nonsense former Labor secretary, and a member of several boards, was a consummate Washington insider. She got right to the point. "Dan," she said, "I need you to come down to the Four Seasons in Georgetown. We are going to dismiss Mr. Raines and several others. Before we do that, we need to know whether you would be willing to serve as the interim CEO." Mudd was speechless. He couldn't believe what he was hearing.

"She said they didn't know whether I was a good guy or a bad guy—or words to that effect," Mudd recalled. "But, at least for the moment, I was all they had, and they needed somebody to be running the place."

Mudd agreed to meet at the Four Seasons restaurant in Georgetown. It was very cloak-and-dagger. Korologos instructed him to go in the side door where someone would meet him, and he went in and waited. When he sat down with Korologos and other board members, he saw that the situation was dire. Fannie Mae was in disarray. There were massive accounting errors, understating losses by about $9 billion over the past three years. Someone had to stick around and clean up the mess, and Mudd was elected.

By then it was questionable whether anyone could turn around the massive enterprise, which had for so many years operated as its own private kingdom, outside the reach of regulators. Raines and his lieutenants were being criticized for amassing personal wealth at the expense of an agency meant to serve average Americans. In 2006 the Office of Federal Housing Enterprise Oversight (OFHEO) filed charges against Raines and two other former executives, alleging fraud and seeking $110 million in penalties and $115 million in returned bonuses. But in a 2008 settlement, the three men agreed to a mere $3 million in fines—and that would be paid by Fannie Mae's insurance company.

The next two years were intense as Mudd supervised the largest restatement that had ever been done, and returned Fannie Mae to responsible accounting practices. Impressed by his work, the board offered to make Mudd permanent CEO. Mudd had always planned to leave once the mess was cleaned up, but he had grown more comfortable with Fannie Mae's culture, and his family loved being in Washington. "Okay," he said, "I'll stay and give it my all."

And then the housing market imploded.

Like every other entity holding mortgage securities, Fannie Mae was forced to address serious issues of liquidity and toxic assets during 2008. By August alarm bells were ringing about how undercapitalized Fannie Mae and Freddie Mac were. Even so, their regulator had given them a pass that summer. Then, right before Labor Day, Mudd received a puzzling letter from the Federal Housing Finance Agency (FHFA) detailing serious capital issues. "The letter basically said, 'I've changed my mind. I now think you have serious capital issues.' It was weird," he told me.

Mudd picked up the phone and called Secretary Paulson, and that was weird, too. "What's going on?" he asked Paulson. "This is different than the good-faith discussion we had two days ago."

"I can't talk," Paulson said. "We're setting up a meeting."

Mudd, accompanied by his board chairman and general counsel, headed over to the FHFA offices for the meeting. As they were standing in the reception area waiting to be called, Ben Bernanke walked in.

"How's it going?" he asked Mudd in a friendly tone.

"Good," Mudd replied. "How's it going with you?"

"Good, good."

"Nice weekend. Weather was pleasant."

As Mudd told me later, "It was totally pathetic. The world was in flames, and we were talking about the weather."

At a meeting upstairs, joined by Paulson, Mudd learned his fate. The federal government was taking over Fannie Mae and Freddie Mac. "We're going to declare conservatorship," Bernanke said, "and we want your whole board to be here tomorrow morning. We need a decision in twenty-four hours, and if you don't want to do it the easy way, we'll do it the hard way."

Just like that, Mudd was out. Over at Freddie Mac, CEO Richard Syron was hearing the same news. It was a done deal.

"Some people thought Fannie was a bit stronger than Freddie;

others thought it wasn't stronger than Freddie. Some even argued that Fannie was weaker than Freddie," a source at the Treasury told me. "So there was some discrepancy in terms of how they stood. But the bottom line was that they were both sufficiently weak, so that as a result of the assets that they were holding, they were going to be in trouble very soon. In fact, they were already in trouble, desperate trouble. So we knew that we were going to be stuck with the bill on Fannie and Freddie. And then the question was what to do with it." Even the most market-oriented people at the Treasury favored conservatorship, because Fannie and Freddie were not full-fledged market institutions anyway.

"It was essentially the worst of both worlds there," my source said. "We had a nonmarket entity with government backing that was behaving badly. I think we all agreed that it was time for those guys to go under. Maybe their role had been important once, but many of us thought they had become obsolete."

Pimco's Mohamed El-Erian put it this way when we discussed it: "The problem was that they tried to run a commercial activity in a noncommercial setting. In the noncommercial setting, there were objectives related to increasing home ownership, with the expectation that loans were fully guaranteed by the government. In the commercial setting, Freddie and Fannie tried to maximize their profits. So you had a noncommercial context with commercial behavior, and as a result it became very unstable. The minute you bring in a noncommercial player, suddenly the incentive changes."

All along Mudd saw it as a structural problem. "Sooner or later, you need to resolve the business model," he told me. "Right up to the end I was saying, 'Let's come up with a new structure.' Because one way or the other, whether you like Dan Mudd or whether you like

Frank Raines, or whether you like any of the leadership, it doesn't matter. There's been a whole series of good, bad, competent, incompetent CEOs running the place. And nobody has found it simple to do. That tells me there's a business-model issue. Let's resolve that, instead of just making it part of the federal government."

A contributory factor to the agencies' problems was the mentality that every American had a right to own a home. This was the American dream, people said, never stopping to question whether such a goal was remotely realistic. The more that home ownership was wrapped in the flag, the worse things grew for the agencies charged with making the dream come true.

On September 7 the government took control of Fannie Mae and Freddie Mac. There was very little controversy about the decision, but there was plenty of unease in the markets. The tentacles of the subprime crisis were extending into nearly every major financial institution. It could not be contained.

The Monday after the takeover of Fannie Mae and Freddie Mac, I interviewed Hank Paulson, searching for clarity. The bailout had fueled a debate about the proper role of government. Was it appropriate to put taxpayers on the line when companies ran into trouble? Hank Paulson, I had learned from experience, was very good at talking lots and saying little, and on this occasion he seamlessly spoke in nonanswers, unruffled and unrevealing—until I asked a question about Lehman Brothers: "Are there plans afoot for a takeover of Lehman?"

He got edgy and jabbed in the direction of his watch. "I've got to hop," he said, suddenly in a rush, and ended our interview. Four days later he would summon the captains of finance to the Federal Reserve for a last-ditch attempt to rescue Lehman.

It was nearly six months to the day since Bear Stearns was snapped up by JPMorgan Chase for a bargain price. Now it was déjà vu all over again—with one difference: how could Lehman have failed to gird itself for this predictable moment? I remembered so vividly the strong sentiment in the financial media and among my sources on Wall Street that the failure of Bear Stearns had set Lehman up for a grand fall. But what could Lehman do now to save itself before the end of a do-or-die weekend?

———

Late on the evening of Friday, September 12, the phone rang in Dick Fuld's office. It was Bank of America's Ken Lewis, the man he most wanted to talk to. He didn't have the phone on speaker, so those in the room heard only his side of the conversation, but it was obvious by his smile and his words that he felt as if he was hearing very good news. Fuld ended the call with, "Ken, I'm looking forward to being your partner. This is going to be a great deal."

He hung up and said, "It's Bank of America. It's going to happen."

Soon after, a source inside Lehman called me on my cell phone. "Bank of America is doing the deal," he said with assurance. "I was in the room when Ken Lewis spoke to Dick. They were basically shaking on it over the phone. Ken gave Dick his home phone number, and they're discussing the details in the morning."

My source was a good one, but was it plausible that Fuld had made a handshake deal with Lewis, even as the heads of JPMorgan, Goldman, Merrill, and others were engaged in a desperate effort to save his company? Maybe he thought he could be a hero cowboy and come riding in with the treasure strapped across his saddle. But the idea that Fuld had overcome Lewis's resistance when Paulson could not sounded bizarre. Was it really happening?

I remained on call late into the evening, trying to stay on top of events at the Federal Reserve. No one expected a resolution on Friday. We all expected a long weekend ahead. When I finally put away my phone and notes, it was long after midnight. I sat back and thought about what I was witnessing.

I was also a citizen, and when I took off my reporter's hat late at night, I gave in to my feelings of sadness that we had come to this point. For a long time the euphoria in the housing market had been troubling, because in my experience, euphoria came before a fall. Now that the fall was happening, I was deeply disappointed and personally shaken. I knew that whatever the outcome of the weekend, things would never again be the same for any of us. There was a lot of pain ahead.

FOUR

Down to the Wire

"Let's say we got together and saved Lehman. Do we then get together and save the next firm and the next firm? And is saving a weak firm undermining our own position in the market?"

—A BANKER IN THE MEETINGS AT THE NEW YORK FEDERAL RESERVE,
RECALLING THE ANXIETY HE AND OTHERS IN THE
ROOM WERE FEELING

SEPTEMBER 13, 2008

Early Saturday morning, I reached the source at Lehman who had alerted me to the late-night phone call between Fuld and Lewis. He was staying at the Michelangelo Hotel, down the street from Lehman's headquarters. "We finished around midnight, so I've only had about five hours of sleep," he said.

"So, do you expect to conclude a deal with Bank of America today?" I asked.

"Yeah, we're done," he said wearily. He sounded more resigned than happy. "So we'll be part of Bank of America. Who cares? At this point I want to say, 'You can have the thing for free.' Whatever. There's no shareholder value left."

"How does Dick Fuld feel about it?"

"Oh, you know Dick," he said with a sad laugh. "Always the optimist."

"Will he survive the sale?"

"Who knows? That's above my pay grade. Look, I've got to run. Talk to you later."

I poured a cup of coffee and kept making calls. One was to my assistant. I was scheduled to fly to Naples, Florida, early Monday for the CME Global Financial Leadership Conference, where I would moderate a panel on the global credit crisis and interview former Fed chairman Paul Volcker. I told my assistant that the trip might have to be canceled, and she should be ready to make other arrangements. I was going to wait and see how things progressed that day.

I called another Lehman source—this one a lower-echelon type who worked below the thirty-first floor. I wanted to get a sense of what the traders were saying. He, too, was heading into the office. Off the record, he confessed to feeling bitter toward Dick Fuld. "It isn't just me," he said. "A lot of us are questioning his judgment and wondering how we got into this mess. Everyone thought Dick walked on water. That was then, this is now. Why did he take so long to try to raise money? Why didn't he see this coming? It's hard to accept."

"What are you being told?" I asked. "Are people saying you should pack up your stuff?"

"No, it's kind of hard to get information. But I'll tell you something. When I came to work for Lehman, it was as if all my dreams had come true. It was the greatest company in the world. So you can imagine how I'm feeling. And multiply that by thousands of others."

———

Ken Lewis, a native of Mississippi, enjoyed being outside the Wall Street club. His roots were lower middle class, and his story had all the elements of a rags-to-riches tale. His entire career had been spent at the Charlotte, North Carolina, headquarters of Bank of America, beginning in 1969, when it was called the North Carolina National Bank. A quiet man who masked his masterful business sense with a low-key Southern charm, he was fond of saying, "New York is a nice place to visit . . . ," leaving no mistake about the ending of the sentence. His office was six-hundred-plus miles from Wall Street, and he liked it like that.

On Saturday morning when he awoke, Lewis had no idea that by morning's end he would be hurtling toward the Big Apple in his private plane, preparing to do the deal of his life. And it wasn't the deal that certain parties had anticipated.

By 7:00 a.m., Lewis was on the phone with Hank Paulson, who was already at work at the Federal Reserve. He told the secretary that the more his people examined Lehman's books, the worse they looked. Paulson replied that the consortium was still debating what they could take on, individually and collectively. He suggested that the consortium might be willing to come up with $40 billion to cover a large part of Lehman's toxic assets. What did Lewis think about that? Lewis was unenthusiastic. He seemed to be retreating further and further from a deal. Once again, Paulson hung up, frustrated with the Bank of America CEO.

The truth was, Lewis had decided he wouldn't buy Lehman. While Dick Fuld may have slept better Friday night thinking he had a verbal agreement with Bank of America, Lewis already knew he had changed course and his company wouldn't be making a deal. How to explain the phone call my source overheard? Maybe Lewis was still making encouraging sounds on Friday, even as he had privately decided against Lehman. But on Saturday morning he was avoiding Fuld's phone calls, as the calls became increasingly frantic. When Fuld phoned the home number Lewis had given him, Lewis's wife, Donna, answered the phone and said Ken wasn't available. Fuld, still thinking he had an agreement with Lewis, and needing to work out the details, pressed Donna Lewis on the urgency, but she remained vague. Her husband, she told Fuld firmly, would have to call him back.

Fuld waited as long as he could before putting in another call to Lewis. This time Donna Lewis sounded testy. "Ken has your message, and he'll call you back if and when he wants to call you back," she said.

Fuld was embarrassed and apologetic. "I'm sorry for disturbing you," he said. "This is the number he gave me, but I won't call again. I'm sorry."

Meanwhile, John Thain awoke Saturday morning with one thought burning in his mind: Protect Merrill. Like Lehman Brothers and Bear Stearns before it, Merrill had its share of risky assets on the books. All the firms did. He was worried about market confidence. What if Lehman fell? Would the ripple effect bring down Merrill? He knew how dangerous the cycle could be. People would say, "Obviously, the assets are not worth what we thought," and down they'd go. He didn't want to be in a position of recovering pennies on the dollar. As he prepared to return to meetings at the Fed, he knew he had to be ready to take action to prevent his own company from losing liquidity if Lehman crashed.

Saturday morning the Federal Reserve was a hive of activity. There were dozens of bankers and lawyers milling around, working at makeshift tables all over the lobby. At 8:00 a.m., Geithner and Paulson were on a conference call with Barclays CEO John Varley and chairman Marcus Agius in London and Bob Diamond at Barclays midtown office. Varley confirmed that Barclays was serious about buying Lehman, but they wanted to leave behind more than $50 billion in bad assets. Paulson judged that they were not bluffing. He wondered if he could convince the CEOs to come up with that number.

When Paulson and Geithner emerged from the call, they headed into the conference room where the Wall Street heads were gathered, a little worse for wear after a short night.

First on the agenda was a report from the group examining Lehman's financials to determine how much money would be needed. Their conclusion: Lehman would have to raise $15 billion to $20 billion to make it out of the hole. This was a stunning amount of money. Remember, JPMorgan bought Bear Stearns for $4 billion. Would anyone pay such big bucks for Lehman? The group examining Lehman's assets had a grim report. The assets were worth about $20 billion less than Lehman had calculated.

The work groups were also finding some egregious examples of how bad it was at Lehman. These examples cut against the sense of entitlement that was prevalent at that time—that Lehman deserved a federal bailout. Clearly the firm had created the dire situation itself. "It was insane," a participant in the meetings told me. "For example, in Dubai you had man-made islands that hadn't been made, and people had bought houses on those islands and secured mortgages for them. But the islands didn't even exist yet! There were a few situations like that and it was just devastating."

A Treasury official who was also in the meetings could not disguise his disgust. "I was pissed off because they were pounding us over our refusal to save Lehman," he told me. "Well, those assholes created the problem."

There were too many holes in Lehman's books, but Paulson urged them on. "We need to know where you guys stand," he said. "If there's a capital hole, the government can't fill it. So how do we get this done?"

The men around the table were feeling the strain. The idea that they would finance a competitor was anathema to them. But the concern went deeper than the question of whether the banks would be altruistic. There were serious long-term practical considerations as well. "Let's say we got together and saved Lehman," one banker speculated. "Do we then get together and save the next firm and the next firm? And is saving a weak firm undermining our own position in the market?"

Lloyd Blankfein was particularly vocal. He assured Paulson that Goldman Sachs would do what was necessary and act responsibly. But what did that mean?

For Thain, the meetings at the Fed were instructive on two counts: First, they convinced him that Lehman would not survive the weekend. The report on the financials confirmed it. Thain was also clear that Lehman's fall would have a devastating effect on other firms, and Merrill was particularly vulnerable.

At one point, Vikram Pandit looked down the length of the long table and pointed at Thain. "Who's going to save them?" he asked. "Everyone knows if Lehman goes down, then it'll be Merrill, and then it'll be Morgan Stanley, and then Goldman."

Thain ignored Pandit's provocative comment, but he was thinking hard about where he could get an infusion of capital. Paulson pulled him aside. The two men knew each other quite well from their shared years at Goldman Sachs. They'd been in tight spots together before. "I think you should call Ken Lewis," Paulson said. He was facing the reality that Lehman had no real franchise value, but Merrill could be saved. "You have the thundering herd," Paulson said with a smile. "Merrill Lynch has a lot of real value."

Thain considered what Paulson was telling him and nodded. "I know what I need to do," he said.

Barely nine months into his term as chief of Merrill Lynch, Thain wasn't thinking about selling the company. He thought he could strike a deal with Ken Lewis for Bank of America to buy a 9 to 10 percent stake in Merrill. That would give Merrill breathing room to get through the crisis of Lehman's fall.

Determined, Thain stepped outside to Liberty Street, pulled his cell phone out of his pocket, and dialed Ken Lewis's number in Charlotte. Lewis immediately took his call, although he'd been unwilling to take Fuld's.

"We should talk," he told Lewis when he reached him. "I think there are some strategic opportunities here."

The two men didn't know each other very well, but they were both speaking for their companies. Lewis, the consummate deal maker, had wanted to buy Merrill Lynch for a long time. Years earlier, Lewis had talked to the leadership of Merrill and had been willing to pay much more for the stock than it was currently trading.

Now, in September 2008, he smelled a bargain. Perhaps this crisis was his opportunity.

"I can be in New York in about three hours," Lewis said.

Saturday afternoon Thain and Lewis sat down together at Lewis's corporate apartment at the Time Warner Center on Columbus Circle. It was just the two of them. Lewis confided to Thain that there would be no deal with Lehman. He'd made the decision the previous evening. Thain proposed that Bank of America buy a minority stake in Merrill—say, 9 or 10 percent.

Lewis shook his head no. "I want one hundred percent," he said. "Or nothing."

———

Quietly, in another room at the Federal Reserve, a separate drama was occurring, with a potential damage far greater than the failure of Lehman or Merrill. It had to do with American International Group (AIG), the mammoth insurance and financial services firm whose tentacles reached into nearly every corner of the economy. As negotiations surrounding Lehman continued hot and heavy on Saturday, Paulson was working on another floor at the Fed, addressing the looming crisis at AIG. Chris Flowers, who had been at the Fed studying Lehman's books on behalf of Bank of America, had also turned his attention to AIG, which he believed was in dire straits. Flowers laid out his papers on the table and began walking Paulson through the numbers. Paulson listened closely, but he was aware that Flowers was by no means a neutral party. Paulson suspected that he was interested in buying pieces of AIG on the cheap, and the board of directors had been resistant.

Paulson and Flowers were former colleagues, too. In fact, it was beginning to feel like old home week for the Goldman Sachs alumni. Flowers had been a partner at Goldman during Paulson's era and was now an incredibly successful private-equity investor who specialized in troubled entities. He was a billionaire who had made *Forbes*'s list of the 400 wealthiest Americans in 2006. Flowers wasn't universally beloved, a reality that troubled him little. He once cheerfully referred to himself as a "low-life grave dancer." He knew who he was. But he was also considered to have a top-notch mind, and it was hard to ignore his analysis when it came to AIG.

"To be honest, AIG was the scariest one of all that weekend," a Treasury Department source told me. "There was no real regulator involved. I mean, insurance was regulated in all fifty states, but there was no common regulator. I remember looking at Hank and saying, 'We're not going to save an insurance company, are we?' He looked at me like I was crazy, because I had no idea the tremendous reach AIG had." Incidentally, I later learned that there were four hundred agencies overseeing AIG, and they all missed the sizeable leverage at the company's financial products division. Four hundred agencies! It wasn't just the Wall Street executives who had dropped the ball. Regulators had messed up royally.

Paulson understood AIG's value all too well. "Every construction project that's insured by AIG will stop tomorrow if they fail," he said. "And the building you live in right now, I guarantee it's insured by AIU Holdings, which is the property and casualty insurance group that's in one hundred twenty countries. And that's only the tip of the iceberg."

In fact, the tentacles of AIG reached into every major country around the globe. It was composed of many insurance companies, covering millions of retirement accounts, life insurance customers, and other entities. Its balance sheet was more than $1 trillion. AIG had made huge investments in credit default swaps to insure mortgage-backed securities.

Paulson picked up the phone and called AIG's CEO, Bob Willumstad. "Come on over," he said. Willumstad and his advisers arrived at 4:30 Saturday and sat down with Paulson, who was feeling the weight of the crisis. He had started out the weekend trying to save Lehman Brothers. Now he had a much bigger problem. AIG was suddenly squeezing all the oxygen out of the building.

———

Hank Greenberg felt an enduring anger that had survived three years of exile from AIG, the company he had built into the largest insurance and financial services enterprise in the world. That anger had only intensified through the mounting financial crisis. Small-framed, but strong and passionate, Greenberg, at eighty-three, had more drive than most men half his age. On Saturday, September 13, he was at his office at C. V. Starr, overlooking Park Avenue. He'd made the decision to stay close to his business that weekend. With so much going on, he felt he'd better stand by. He was aware that AIG was having trouble, and that Willumstad was trying to arrange a meeting with the feds to make the case for a loan because he had been unsuccessful in raising funds on the outside. Greenberg knew something very few people appreciated at that point—that a failure at AIG would make the Lehman collapse look like a day at the beach.

As he drank tea from delicate china cups, studied reports, and made calls, Greenberg considered how the people at AIG were handling the crisis. He was not pleased. They weren't thinking! They were desperate, and he knew from long experience that desperation was fatally contagious. The one thing you had to do, he believed, when all around you was going awry, was to keep your wits about you and stay calm. You didn't react to a crisis by becoming part of the crisis, but by stepping away from it, viewing it dispassionately, and making decisions from a place of objectivity.

Greenberg had to work hard himself at maintaining that dispassionate view. He wasn't usually an overly emotional person, but he was emotional about AIG. The company was his life's work, the canvas upon which he produced his vision, and it had succeeded brilliantly. After Greenberg took the reins from the founder and his mentor, Cornelius Vander Starr, in 1968, he had put AIG on the map, breaking into hard-fought markets like China and Russia long before others did. Too crusty to be personally popular, Greenberg was nonetheless admired for his business acumen. But he was also feared. When he was at his peak at AIG, everyone knew you didn't cross Hank Greenberg.

Then, in 2005, crusading New York attorney general Eliot Spitzer went after Greenberg with accusations of accounting fraud. The allegations would never be proved and were later dropped, but the mere hint of wrongdoing was enough to panic AIG's board. With barely a thought, Greenberg was forced out and replaced by Martin Sullivan, a fifty-year-old British-born executive who worked for Greenberg. Believing Sullivan had helped drive him out, Greenberg never felt the same about him again, but even without the personal animosity, there was no question Sullivan was ill-equipped to run a global insurance powerhouse. From his new perch as the head of the financial services firm C. V. Starr & Co., and as one of AIG's largest stockholders, Greenberg watched with alarm as the new management made one bad decision after another. In June 2008 Sullivan was ousted and replaced by Willumstad, a former lieutenant of Sandy Weill's at Citigroup. Willumstad had gotten along well with Greenberg and had also been backed by Greenberg's powerful ally Eli Broad. (Greenberg's AIG had purchased Broad's asset-management company, SunAmerica, in 1999.) Willumstad talked about repairing the relationship with Greenberg once he became CEO—something Greenberg was eager to do. He wanted to help AIG. To be clear, Greenberg wasn't just being altruistic or paternalistic. His personal wealth was completely tied up in AIG, and it was sinking with the stock price. But so far Willumstad had shut him out, not returning his calls.

Greenberg also had a reason to follow Lehman Brothers closely. Back in June 2008, when others were pulling away from Lehman, Greenberg took a chance on the firm, making a substantial investment. He'd called Lehman "a great franchise" and predicted the end of the real estate crisis. Now he was watching his investment turn to dust, and he wanted to be involved in a solution. Over the course of the weekend, Greenberg spoke with Dick Fuld several times. Fuld, hunkered down in his office across town, outlined the possibilities as he saw them but told Greenberg that he believed a deal would be struck with Bank of America. Greenberg noticed during those conversations with Fuld that Lehman's chief had absolute confidence that Lehman Brothers would survive. He didn't sound desperate or afraid.

As for AIG, Greenberg was deeply concerned but not surprised that it had reached a crisis point. I had interviewed him in June, right after Martin Sullivan was replaced by Bob Wil-lumstad. It seemed that since Greenberg had been pushed out, AIG had suffered a crisis of leadership. The price of stock fell by half in one year, and the company was suffering $13 billion in losses and another $30 billion in write-downs. It was deeply upsetting to Greenberg. "Shareholders are disgusted," he said, speaking for himself and others. "You can't have a company as great as AIG was in market value—the highest of any insurance company in history—suddenly become a basket case." He added pointedly, "You have to ask yourself, where was the board in all this period of time? The board elevated its fees by three times, literally, for all the, quote 'hard work they were doing' unquote. Well, you don't have to be a rocket scientist to figure out things are going badly."

I looked at him intently. I could feel the frustration radiating off his slender shoulders. "AIG operates in a hundred and thirty countries," I said. "You built this company. Some people say there's no one who can really control this behemoth other than you, given your intimate knowledge of the firm."

He smiled thinly. "I've heard people say that, and I think it's silly. There's more than one person in the world that can run a company. You've got to have an individual who has the vision, the energy, who is willing to pay the price, which means working 24/7—and you don't do it because you have to, you do it because you love to . . ."

This was a familiar theme of my conversations with Greenberg. He took it personally. Now, with his old company on the rocks, he desperately wished he were at the helm so he could steer the ship to safety. Instead, he was shut out and shut down, and he feared what each day's news cycle would bring.

By Saturday afternoon the complexion of the crisis had changed. When I heard that Ken Lewis was talking to John Thain, I knew that Lehman was down to one suitor. It was all happening with dizzying speed. Obviously, Thain didn't go into that weekend with the intention of selling his firm, but that's what seemed to be happening. For his part, it was startling to me how quickly Ken Lewis was able to orchestrate a deal. He hadn't gone into the weekend expecting to buy Merrill Lynch, either.

I reached out to a source at Lehman, wondering how Fuld was handling the news.

"Dick is amazing," he told me. "He must be pissed as hell, but you'd never know it. He's shifting all his attention to Barclays, and he thinks it will happen."

The CEOs, hard at work at the Fed, were operating on that premise. Their task was to figure out how to plug the gap. Everything was on the table. Could Barclays put in a little more? "It looked like we could get something done," UBS's Robert Wolf told me. "If Barclays would take on more of the [bad] assets, then we'd put together a new company of the leftover assets and the Street would own it. We were very focused, and no one had time to sit back and say, 'What does this next step mean, or worse, what will it mean if Lehman actually fails?' We only had until Sunday."

As it became clear that Bank of America was out of the running for Lehman, Bob Diamond of Barclays was still working the financials. By late afternoon he thought there might be a deal. Paulson burned up the lines with Barclays CEO John Varley in London. Barclays was the only potential buyer left, and there were problems.

By law Barclays had to have a shareholder vote on such a major purchase, and that could take thirty to sixty days. Diamond and Varley were pressuring Paulson. Would the federal government guarantee a purchase until then? Paulson knew there was no way he could do that.

Paulson was concerned about the number of roadblocks the British were putting up. The regulators were brutal. "It's like they don't want to catch the American disease," Paulson observed to an aide.

Yet at day's end, Barclays was still in there. It was a last-minute reprieve. Everyone breathed a sigh of relief as the word spread that Barclays had agreed to buy Lehman—on the condition that the sale would not include bad real estate assets. But there was complete uncertainty about what would happen. Late Saturday evening, a Lehman executive walked into a conference room and saw several sheets of paper lined up on the table. They were press releases. One press release announced a sale to Bank of America. Another announced a sale to Barclays. Another announced that Lehman had found a halo investor in the Middle East. One announced a bank consortium had purchased Lehman's real estate assets. He stared at the press releases and thought, "No one knows which one will be released—or, worse, if the press release that isn't here, the one announcing bankruptcy, will be the outcome." He backed out of the conference room, not wanting to look.

FIVE

Death Sentence
and Champagne

"This company's going to be a thing of beauty as we get to the other side of this economic downturn. It will be the envy of the financial services industry."

—KEN LEWIS, CEO OF BANK OF AMERICA, IN AN INTERVIEW WITH
MARIA BARTIROMO, SEPTEMBER 15, 2008

SEPTEMBER 14, 2008

By Sunday morning I realized that the developments in New York were so significant that I couldn't leave to attend the CME conference. I sent my regrets to the chairman, Terrence Duffy. He was quite understanding. I was hardly the only one to bail on his conference. In fact, when Paul Volcker gave the keynote Monday afternoon to a half-filled room, he joked, "I want to congratulate you for the timing of this conference."

On Sunday I was following two tracks. The first and most significant was the fate of Lehman Brothers. I could feel the tick, tick, ticking of this time bomb as we headed into the final twelve hours. The deadline was set for the opening of the Asian markets. The second track was the emerging—and unexpected—story of a developing agreement between Bank of America and Merrill Lynch. I got ready for a busy day.

Bob Diamond and his team had worked through the night, trying to put together the pieces of the deal. It was 4:00 a.m. before they left the Fed, and Diamond didn't go to bed. He had a call scheduled with his board; it was 10:00 a.m. in London. He was sleepy but optimistic. All that remained was for the deal to be sent to the British regulatory body, the Financial Services Authority, for its approval. But the call jolted him—and not in a good way. For the first time he was hearing that the FSA was probably going to reject the purchase, even if the consortium covered Lehman's bad debt. It was, they felt, just too risky. Diamond knew that he wouldn't be getting any sleep.

It wasn't just the failure of his arduous efforts over the past few days that upset Diamond, or even the prospect of not getting Lehman, which he wanted more than his superiors, his board, or the British government. He felt blindsided and embarrassed. His counterparts had expected him to act in good faith, and he had, but he knew it wouldn't look that way on the Street.

At 8:00 a.m. Diamond joined a conference call with Geithner and Paulson at the Fed, and John Varley in London. Varley broke the news to Geithner and Paulson that the FSA was balking. They were shocked but immediately went into action. Geithner placed a call to Callum McCarthy, the FSA chairman. McCarthy repeated the British government's concern that they would be taking on too much risk. He didn't exactly say no, but he asked for more time for due diligence, and there just wasn't any. He also mentioned the requirement that Barclays' shareholders vote on big acquisitions and said that if the American government could cover Lehman for thirty to sixty days prior to a vote, maybe they could do the deal.

Geithner already knew that was impossible, but it also made absolutely no sense. Let's say the federal government lent Lehman Brothers enough to carry it for sixty to ninety days. Investors would surely bolt in large numbers in response to the uncertainty, and the problems with Lehman's balance sheet would grow much worse. By the time the Barclays shareholders considered a purchase, it would be a real mess, and they would likely say no. It just wasn't going to happen.

Paulson got on the phone with Chancellor of the Exchequer Alistair Darling, whose response was chilly. He asked Paulson why the British government and taxpayers should take on Lehman's problems if the American government would not.

Paulson got it but he was deeply disappointed. "They kind of strung us along," one of Paulson's aides told me. "It felt like the British government never had any intention of doing this deal without a promise from the American government, which Hank could not give. We had been living on pure adrenaline for days, and now we felt deflated. It was awful."

As noon approached, it became clear that the British would not budge. It was over.

Paulson retreated to a private office and called Fuld. "Dick," he said, "I feel terrible about this, but the British government is not going to approve the sale. We're out of options."

"No!" Fuld cried. "You've got to do something." But there was nothing that could be done. Fuld looked out of his office where board members had begun drifting onto the thirty-first floor, waiting while executives continued working on a Barclays deal. When the word came down that the British government said a sale to Barclays was too risky, all the wind went out of their efforts. Now what?

A source told me, "You know, this whole weekend has been a roller coaster—'We're done.' 'We're not done.' 'We're done.' 'We're not done.' Now we really were done."

At the Federal Reserve, unaware of the drama, the CEOs were working on an arrangement to put up $30 billion. It was a remarkable act of collaboration—and, one may even say, of generosity. To be sure, they all felt jeopardized by the prospect of a Lehman failure, but it was still impressive that they were able to finalize such a huge commitment in less than two days.

At 1:00 p.m., Paulson, Geithner, and Cox entered the room. Paulson delivered the news to the CEOs. "The British screwed us," he said. Christopher Cox said he had notified Dick Fuld that Lehman should file for bankruptcy.

"I actually thought there was going to be a solution for Lehman, up until the moment there wasn't," BlackRock's Larry Fink told me. "At one time during the weekend it felt as if everything was going to be resolved. Everybody said Lehman was too big to fail. But we didn't have time to figure it out."

Word of a pending bankruptcy was leaking out to Lehman employees, and the fear and uncertainty were tremendous. "People don't know what to expect on Monday," a source inside the company told me. "They're talking about wearing jeans to work. They don't know if they'll have jobs." Managers were trying to still the panic. Someone later e-mailed me a copy of a message that went out from a manager on Sunday afternoon:

> **Team:**
> **Given the recent press reports regarding Lehman, I wanted to communicate that we are counting on you to be at work on Monday and ready for business as usual. In fact, I ask that you take the extra time necessary to coordinate with your teams to conduct a "ready for business" check on all mission critical activities before the day begins. Thanks as always for your commitment.**

Things were a little better over at Merrill Lynch, where the final details of an agreement between John Thain and Ken Lewis were being worked out—although many people did not know what to make of a sale to Bank of America and what it would mean to them. The terms surprised me a bit. This was no fire sale. At $29 a share, it looked as if Bank of America was paying a huge premium, since Merrill had closed Friday at $17.05. Clearly, Lewis really wanted to own Merrill Lynch.

When I learned that there would be a press conference at Bank of America's New York offices Monday morning, I reached out to Lewis, hoping to do a one-on-one afterward. My producer Lulu Chiang had cameras at the press conference and followed up on the interview with Lewis.

At the Federal Reserve, Chris Cox and a team of lawyers were outlining the basic mechanics of bankruptcy to Lehman's people. The SEC had a role to play in bankruptcy, but only as a facilitator. He couldn't force Fuld to declare. "It's important that you make an announcement before the Asian markets open [8:00 p.m. Sunday,

New York time]," he told Fuld. But Lehman was dragging its feet. Watching the clock, Cox grew increasingly concerned. Finally, at 8:00 p.m., with Lehman's board gathered, Cox put in a call. "It's time for you to do the right thing," he said.

The board wasn't sure what he meant. "Are you telling us to go into bankruptcy?" one member asked.

"No," Cox hedged, "I'm telling you what the situation is." As their regulator, he couldn't order them to go into bankruptcy, but he was letting them know that they were out of options.

An executive who was on the call told me, "There was no doubt what the intention was. And the Lehman board was scared and shocked. It was a very big deal." He added that everyone thought Cox had stepped over the line by calling the board. "Our board was outraged that Cox butted into the board meeting. That had never been done before. Everyone's nerves were so frayed that they briefly let anger get the better of them."

It took Lehman until 1:45 a.m., long after the Asian markets had opened, to declare bankruptcy.

A Treasury official acknowledged to me the difficulty of the outcome but defended the Treasury's stance on Lehman. "People have said, 'But why couldn't you have done something to facilitate a purchase? They forget that everyone who might be a potential buyer knew how bad things were at Lehman. Companies weren't jumping up and down, saying, 'Let me buy it!' They weren't lined up outside the door saying, 'I'd buy Lehman if only the government would help me.' If you have no buyer, you have no buyer. The government can't compel someone to buy."

Many people were confused on this point. What was the proper role of the federal government. "For one thing," a source in Washington explained, "the Treasury just didn't have the money to rescue institutions. This was before Congress authorized TARP [Troubled Asset Relief Program] funds. The Treasury couldn't buy or bail out institutions. It wasn't a question of whether Hank Paulson wanted to do it or not."

Another source in the Treasury spoke with me, the sadness and frustration clear in his voice. "It wasn't like a decision was made on Friday that these guys were just doomed and we were going to let them go. There was an attempt over that entire weekend to save them. And the fact is, we didn't. So in that sense it was a failure, and once Barclays pulled out, we didn't have any other options. We didn't have the legal authority to do anything differently. So, I don't blame us for failing that weekend. I blame the fact that we didn't have mechanisms set up in advance to deal with these sorts of contingencies." He sighed and added, "It would be great if we were all smarter, but we're not."

Late Sunday, September 14, the CEOs pulled their chairs back from the table and began to pack their briefcases. They had failed at the core mission of the weekend, which was to save Lehman Brothers. But their minds were elsewhere. "When we walked out of there Sunday night, a few of us commented that there was still a big elephant in the room," one of them told me. "And that was AIG. When we mentioned AIG to Geithner, he kind of brushed us off, saying, 'Yeah, we're taking care of that, but it's not part of this discussion.' Some of us disagreed. We thought if there was an announcement that Lehman went under, but Merrill was saved and AIG was taken care of, maybe the markets wouldn't be so negatively affected. But with the big elephant of AIG still in the room, no one felt at ease."

It was well into the evening when I reached a source at Lehman

Brothers. The adrenaline shot provided by hope had worn off, and he was dragging with exhaustion. He could spare me only a minute because he was immersed in the details of the bankruptcy filing. "This is my family," he said, and I could hear his tears. "What's going to happen to my assistants, my secretary? So many people will be hurt by this. We failed them. *I* failed them." There was silence on the line for a moment, and then he said, "I feel terrible."

Near midnight, John Thain, Ken Lewis, and their teams were lifting champagne glasses, toasting the deal. Had they been able to foretell the future, they might have held off on the bubbly.

SIX

Fallout

"Those of us who have looked to the self-interest of lending institutions to protect shareholders' equity, myself included, are in a state of shocked disbelief."

—ALAN GREENSPAN IN CONGRESSIONAL TESTIMONY, OCTOBER 2008

SEPTEMBER 15, 2008

An image played in Win Smith's mind as he watched the news of the sale of Merrill Lynch: a thundering herd of bulls storming over the horizon, joyfully kicking up huge clouds of dust as their giant hooves pounded into the earth. That was his Merrill, the company he loved, the company his father had joined in 1916 with the founders, Charlie Merrill and Eddie Lynch, to bring Wall Street to Main Street, a goal they achieved with bullish determination. But there was a second image Smith held in his mind, distinctly different but every bit as essential—the benevolent visage of "Mother Merrill," the good soul of the firm. For if a firm could be said to have a soul, it was Merrill Lynch.

Winthrop Smith Jr., fifty-five, had personally known every Merrill CEO, from Charlie Merrill to John Thain—although he didn't know Thain well. He grew up hearing the iconic tales of "Mother Merrill" at his father's knee—how Merrill warned its clients to sell ahead of the crash of 1929, thus rescuing their investments; or of the time in the 1970s when a stock Merrill recommended crashed and CEO Don Regan (future secretary of the Treasury and then chief of staff in the Reagan administration) said outright, "We goofed," and made investors whole. These were the stories everyone at Merrill loved to tell, believing they belonged to a unique bastion of virtue at the craven heart of Wall Street.

Smith had spent twenty-eight years there himself, rising to become executive vice president and chairman of Merrill Lynch International before leaving in 2001. Stan O'Neal had just been named chairman and CEO, and Smith was offered the vice chairmanship but declined to stay. Seven years later, he still felt so much pride in the company and its people. He had loved the underdog feistiness of Merrill, the strong leadership and warm heart that had characterized it for most of its history. Now Merrill's motto, "We're bullish on the future," seemed like a relic of the past.

It was sad to say good-bye. But for Win Smith, the emotional end had come much, much earlier. He did not believe that the current subprime crisis had brought Merrill down. In the months and years preceding the sale, Smith had made no secret of his anger toward one man, who he believed was responsible for ruining a great company: Stan O'Neal, the CEO who had been forced out in 2007.

Smith was openly bitter about O'Neal's tenure and the damage it had done to Merrill. Although O'Neal had received positive press as the grandson of a former slave and the first African American to run a major Wall Street firm, he was responsible for moving Merrill away from its core business into the lucrative (and ultimately fatal) subprime market. And then, much like Dick Fuld, he had failed to see the path of destruction until Merrill was already shaken. Shortly before his ouster in 2007, O'Neal told investors that the subprime problem was "reasonably well contained. There have been no clear signs that it is spilling over into other subsets of the bond market, the fixed income market, and the credit market." He was wrong about that, of course, but being wrong did not prevent O'Neal from taking away a compensation package worth $161.5 million when he left. In Win Smith's view, it was highway robbery.

There were those on the Street who said Smith's anger was really just sour grapes, since O'Neal had beaten him out for the top job. I once asked Smith if that was true, and if O'Neal's poor reception and ultimate ouster was a case of the old guard at Merrill taking aim at an outsider. He denied it vehemently. "What he did that made many of us nonsupportive was to publicly castigate Mother Merrill without understanding what Mother Merrill stood for," he said. "It was really a culture built around five principles: [Number one,] the client's interests must come first. Second, one was to respect one's colleagues. Third, the firm relied on teamwork. Fourth, you had a responsibility to your communities. And fifth was integrity: you never did anything that you couldn't read about on the front page of the *Wall Street Journal*. I don't think those principles were something Stan embraced or articulated. He thought Mother Merrill stood for paternalism—softness—which it did not in any way."

He admitted that he was disappointed to have been passed over as CEO. "Would I have loved to have had the job? Absolutely. Would I have totally supported any of the candidates if they had not taken the firm in a direction with which I didn't agree? Absolutely.

So no, I'm not bitter. I just do not agree with what O'Neal did, and I certainly don't agree with the way he maligned a culture that had worked for almost ninety years."

Now Smith watched the events unfolding that would bring an end to Merrill's magnificent reign. He knew the sale was necessary. He was ready to support John Thain. But it felt like a death in the family.

———

I awoke hours before dawn on Monday morning and left the house at 5:45 for an early appearance on the *Today* show, which would be filmed live from the floor of the New York Stock Exchange. The overnight news, as expected, was terrible. The foreign markets were sliding. It would be a long day for me as I tried to stay on top of developments. This was phase one of the crisis, characterized by panic and speculation. It would take several days to get a sensible picture—that is, assuming there were no new calamities in store. Over the weekend, Hurricane Ike had wrought devastation in Galveston, Texas. The analogies to the financial storm on Wall Street were inescapable.

At 7:00 a.m., reporting from the NYSE, I tried to cobble together the outline of the facts. It was clear to me at that point that the Merrill sale to Bank of America was as big a story as the fall of Lehman Brothers, because it provided a window into the questions on everyone's mind: What happens next? Was it a precursor of more trouble to come?

After the *Today* show, I headed over to Bank of America headquarters, where Ken Lewis and John Thain were scheduled to give a

10:00 a.m. press conference. The first thing I noticed when the two men walked into the room and shook hands for the camera was the awkward body language. They were not comfortable with each other, or, I suspected, entirely confident about the giant leap they had made over the course of a single weekend. Thain's face looked gray with fatigue, and his standard close-mouthed smile seemed more strained than usual. I could see in his eyes that he felt defeated. Sitting side by side in their dark suits and red ties, sipping water from glasses embossed with the Bank of America logo, they were an odd couple. Lewis's opening statement—"We thought this was the strategic opportunity of a lifetime"—might have seemed more plausible if the financial world wasn't in upheaval. Thain added that his own people inside Merrill were delighted with the deal, glossing over what must have been incredible turmoil and uncertainty at Merrill.

I thought it interesting that early on in the press conference reporters phrased their questions as if assuming that Bank of America and Merrill had been talking about a deal for weeks, although the agreement was nailed down only over the weekend. Lewis and Thain both looked a bit abashed when they admitted that prior to Saturday morning there had been no discussion between them about a purchase. It was unbelievably fast. Why not just wait? Why buy Merrill at such a premium? I wasn't the only one wondering what was going on. Surely, after the Lehman news, Merrill's stock would have been under pressure, and Lewis could have picked it up cheaper.

Toward the end of the press conference there was an odd note when a reporter asked Thain what his role would be in the new merger. His face went blank for a second before he murmured, "To be honest, I haven't had a chance to flesh out that discussion." Lewis smiled approvingly, calling Thain selfless. "It was never about him," he said. "It was always about the deal." In the months ahead I would have reason to think about this many times.

As the room cleared after the press conference, I sat down to tape a lengthier one-on-one with Lewis, which would air on *Closing Bell*. I wanted to pursue the question of due diligence—how such a major deal could be struck in a forty-eight-hour period. Did he really have the time to study Merrill's books? He replied in a very relaxed manner—essentially saying, "Not to worry. We know what we're doing."

I was also curious about the man himself. Lewis had told me on many occasions that investment banking was too volatile, and he definitely didn't want to be in that business. "You are in that business now in a big way," I observed. "What changed?"

He tried to sell me on a new vision of a company that married the two strongest factions of the financial industry to form an unbeatable entity. "It will be the envy of the financial services industry in terms of market share," he said. "And the power with which we can operate in the best country in the world. If you want to create that formidable company, you have to be opportunistic."

There was no doubt in my mind that Lewis was optimistic. He saw the purchase as an amazing opportunity, a real coup. He leaned toward me, forcefully making his point. "This company's going to be a thing of beauty as we get to the other side of this economic downturn," he insisted. "It will be the envy of the financial services industry."

I left my interview with Lewis and headed back downtown to prepare for my show at the New York Stock Exchange. I needed time to think and study, but events were happening too fast to allow an opportunity for reflection. Complicating matters was the fact that we were in the final weeks of an intensely fought presidential campaign. Ticking across the wire was a statement by Republican nominee John McCain, obviously trying to quell panic, saying, "The fundamentals of our economy are strong." It was one of those devastating remarks that continued to echo long into the campaign. The debate McCain's remark generated had to do with what the fundamentals actually were. But there was no escaping it. Everywhere you looked there was a meltdown. Wall Street was getting the stuffing kicked out of it, and the stakes were no less than the future of the entire U.S. economy.

I worked my BlackBerry lining up guests and gathering information. "Let's get Win Smith to talk about his reaction to the Merrill deal," I suggested to my producer. "And find out if Meredith Whitney is available."

Closing Bell was a packed show that day. Win Smith was my first guest. Smith was not one to grab the spotlight, but more than almost anyone I could think of, he represented the Merrill founders. He had a dog in this fight, if only because of his father's service. "What are your thoughts?" I asked him. His words were measured but his voice sounded grief stricken. "As I've gone though the day I've had three types of emotions," he said. "First, I feel very, very sad—my family is sad; the Merrill families are sad. On the other hand, there's relief. Things could have been much worse. Thain made a good deal with Bank of America."

And the third emotion?

"Frankly, I feel a lot of anger," Smith said. "I feel a lot of anger for the former CEO Stan O'Neal, and for the board of directors, who really acted incredibly irresponsibly and got us into this position and dealt John the hand that he was dealt today."

I had no doubt that Win Smith would have plenty more to say as the dust settled and the full implications of the merger took hold—and that turned out to be true. However, with all the turmoil swirling around us that day, Merrill seemed more like a winner than a loser. We had to look at the entities that may still fall in the coming weeks and months, the state of insecurity of the system as a whole, and whether a greater collapse was imminent. Meredith Whitney of Oppenheimer, who had been calling it right during this period, had been one of the first to start issuing warnings about the consequences of overleveraging years earlier when people should have paid heed. She never minced words or offered standard pap. She was often the first one out with the bad news, which earned her the informal title of the new "ax" on Wall Street. (One of Whitney's best calls was that Citigroup would be forced to cut its dividend, which happened weeks after she predicted it and caused the stock to plummet.)

Whitney was completely unsentimental about Wall Street. She called it as she saw it, and on September 15 she was already looking ahead to the next upheavals and failures, specifically naming Wachovia, Washington Mutual, and Citibank as being vulnerable. (In retrospect, her predictions would prove to be 100 percent true.) By the time the closing bell rang at 4:00 p.m. on Monday, the Dow had dropped 500 points, the largest drop in seven years.

Throughout the day the news cameras focused on the volatile scene taking place at Lehman Brothers, as stunned workers carried boxes of their belongings out through the revolving doors. Most of them looked shell-shocked. Some were blistering with anger. At one point during the day, a group erected a giant picture of Dick Fuld outside the building, and employees scribbled comments like, "Thanks for screwing up." Tourists gathered, pointing digital cameras at the scene and having their pictures taken under the Lehman logo.

One source said to me on Monday, "I wasn't here in 1929, but I'm pretty sure it felt like what it feels like today."

Back in Washington, Hank Paulson held a press conference in the West Wing briefing room. He knew what to expect. People wanted to understand the difference between Bear Stearns and Lehman Brothers. And they wanted to know if the Lehman collapse was a message from the government that there would be no more help coming from Washington. At the press conference, Paulson insisted that Lehman Brothers' circumstances were different than Bear Stearns', and voiced a sentiment likely to be well received on Capitol Hill: "I never once considered it appropriate to put taxpayer money on the line in resolving Lehman Brothers."

Literally every player across the board in the financial system was scrambling to secure its own interests. "Our days had been starting at two a.m. for a couple of weeks," Mohamed El-Erian recalled. "The weekend of Lehman we were in all of Saturday, all of Sunday. We had plan A, plan B, and plan C. Plan A was that you'd get a repeat of Bear Stearns, so at the very last minute you'd have a marriage of some sort—like the Barclays-Lehman solution. Plan B was that Lehman failed, but in an orderly fashion, so that someone in the government minimized the shock to the payments and settlement system. And plan C was that Lehman failed in a disorderly fashion.

"We had responses for A, B, and C. We were ready. And it

became clear on Sunday that it was going to be C. Very early on Monday morning we sent lawyers to deliver notices of default to Lehman, which then allowed us to crystallize whatever swap positions we had and to replace them pretty quickly so that our clients would be protected. We then went around to make sure that every aspect of the business was robust enough to weather the upcoming storm. It took a few days for the whole thing to play out. We had to find out where every dollar of our cash was, who our counterparties were, who had our collateral. And there was a heightened sense that we could no longer take a single thing for granted. We got very defensive very quickly. We raised cash, and we made sure that everybody understood that no matter what they were seeing in their sector, the massive liquidity shock was the overriding issue. We canceled vacations completely. It was all hands on deck. There was a lot more communication with clients, because a lot of our clients—and we have eight million of them—didn't know what was going on at all. There was a massive increase in the amount of communication with the outside world."

That scene was duplicated across the financial landscape, on a global level. "The week of September 15, everything halted," El-Erian said. "And it happened in a cascading and a rapidly accelerating fashion. It was the equivalent of what the economists call a sudden stop to markets. It's like a cardiac arrest, where it doesn't matter whether you're the leg or the arm—if the heart stops, everything stops. So what you got, starting on the Monday, but really building up to Wednesday and Thursday of that week, was a cascading cardiac arrest of the system. We saw it on the trading floor, where area after area simply could not get things done. It didn't matter if you were the creditor or the debtor on the transaction, you couldn't get it done. And that's because the trust in the payments and settlement system evaporated. So no one wanted to take any risk.

"Here's an analogy. I live in California, and we have the most efficient fast-food drive-through system in the country. You put your order in, you go to the first window to pay, and then to the second window to collect your food, and you're out of there in thirty seconds. It works very well. Now, imagine what would happen if you went up to your McDonald's drive-though, put in your order, and went to the first window. What if when they asked for your five dollars, you said, 'Where's my Big Mac?' And they said, 'Your Big Mac is down at the second window.' But you weren't sure if you believed them, because that day you'd heard that the system broke down at a nearby Burger King, and a lot of people paid for their food but found that the second window was closed. So you didn't trust that you'd find your Big Mac at the second window. You pulled out of line and went away hungry. You had the money, and you were willing to transact, but you didn't have the confidence that allowed a transaction to happen. Eventually, even though McDonald's was able to feed people, and even though customers were willing and able to make transactions, the whole system collapsed. And that's what started to happen in the financial system. It started slowly on Monday, and then really accelerated on Wednesday. The system seized up very quickly."

It would be late in the evening before I finally arrived home, exhausted but buzzed. The day had been dubbed "Black Monday," but it felt like black-and-blue Monday to me. I had hours of study ahead of me, another early morning report for the *Today* show, and my own show at the NYSE later that day. I felt the need to bring clarity to a situation that was messy and unstable. I had learned that

117

while the press was focused on the fates of Lehman Brothers and Merrill Lynch that day, behind the scenes the Feds were scrambling to prevent a major catastrophe brewing at AIG. And unbeknownst to most people, Bob Diamond was still studying Lehman.

———

The canniness of Bob Diamond was never more evident than on Tuesday, September 16. Diamond had gone into the weekend wanting Lehman, and now he was on a scavenger hunt. Even as pictures of stockbrokers forming a funeral procession out the building doors filled the television screens, Diamond and his Barclays team were at Lehman looking at what they could buy postbankruptcy. Although this was an incredibly sad day for many people, it also represented a great opportunity for Diamond, and he was not going to let it pass him by.

On Wednesday, Barclays announced a $1.75 billion purchase of Lehman's North American investment banking business, which would potentially save the jobs of up to ten thousand Lehman workers. Included in the price was Lehman's Time Square building, a dazzling thirty-two-floor structure whose flashing LED screens often stopped passersby in their tracks. The facility had trading floors and technology ready to open for business immediately. Prior to purchasing the Times Square building, Lehman was housed in the World Financial Center, a complex across from the World Trade Center that suffered substantial damage on 9/11. Lehman's data center and trading floor were destroyed. Rather than waiting to see what would happen with the location, Lehman moved quickly to purchase the building at 745 Seventh Avenue in October 2001.

Originally built by Morgan Stanley, it had the advantage of being prefitted with state-of-the-art technology and architecture for the trading business. Now it would belong to Barclays, and it was ready for a seamless transaction—just turn on the lights and go. Like it or not, it was an amazing coup for Diamond and for Barclays.

Diamond and Lehman president Bart McDade (who was offered a job with Barclays) visited the trading floors and met personally with the staff, calming jangled nerves and urging everyone to put emotions behind them.

On Wednesday I sat down with Diamond to ask him some questions about the surprising Barclays deal. "I'm trying to figure out how this all plays out," I said to him. "Let me ask you this: Do you feel any guilt at not rescuing all of Lehman?" It was an uncomfortable question, and Diamond conceded, "We were—we were, you know, quite fortunate. Because of the bank we were able to just select those assets and liabilities that fit with the business we were taking." He added that Barclays rightly did not want to take on any risk, and without a federal backstop, a deal for the whole purchase was just out of the question. But this limited purchase allowed Barclays to get a foothold in the United States. In many respects it was a brilliant deal. As we spoke, just days after Lehman declared bankruptcy, the Lehman sign was coming off the building and a Barclays sign was going up.

The immediate fallout of the weekend's events—at least where Merrill and Lehman were concerned—was starting to wrap up. But anyone who believed that the crisis was about the future of a couple of investment banking firms wasn't seeing the bigger picture. Indeed, the symbol of the crisis in the months to come would not be

Lehman, Merrill, or even Bear Stearns, but AIG, which, like Fannie and Freddie before it, became the company deemed too big to fail.

By Tuesday, September 16, all eyes were on AIG, and the news was emerging that the Feds were discussing an $85 billion bailout of the troubled insurance giant.

———

The force of his personality gave David Boies a youthful demeanor that belied his sixty-seven years. He was one of the most successful and well-known lawyers in America, whose career included a number of landmark cases. In the presidential election of 2000, Boies had achieved great notoriety, appearing on the news and talk shows to defend the interests of his client Al Gore during the dispute over the Florida-vote tally. He lost that battle but remained engaged in many high-profile cases. In 2005 he began representing Hank Greenberg, and now he was carrying his banner into the media battle. Boies appeared on *Closing Bell* waving a copy of the letter Greenberg had sent Bob Willumstad on Tuesday, after AIG's credit rating was downgraded Monday by Standard & Poor's and Moody's. The stock dropped by 61 percent on Monday, and the slide would continue the next day. This was a stunning fall for the venerable company. The situation was so dire that Monday the Feds once again knocked on the doors of Jamie Dimon and Lloyd Blankfein. Could JPMorgan and Goldman Sachs put together a $75 billion line of credit to save AIG?

Boies explained that in the midst of the approaching calamity, his client, Hank Greenberg, had made repeated offers to help. Indeed, his history with the company and his position as its largest shareholder positioned him perfectly to do so. Boies described the letter Greenberg had written to Willumstad as a kind of final appeal that had also been ignored. I perused the text of the letter and found it quite extraordinary. In part it read:

> Dear Bob:
>
> We have been discussing for several weeks my offer to assist the company in any way that you and the Board desired. Throughout these discussions, you have told me and David Boies that you believed that my assistance was important to the company. The only concern that you have expressed to me is the fear that if I were to become an advisor to the company that I would "overshadow" you. I respectfully suggest to you, and to the Board, that the continuing refusal to work together to save this great company is far more important than any concern over personal positions or perceptions.
>
> In little over a year, I and other shareholders, have watched the company that I helped build over 35 years into the largest and most successful insurance company in history and one of the most profitable financial companies in the world lose over 90% of its value . . . Over the last two weeks as the threats to the company increased, I have made repeated requests to meet with you and to meet with the Board to offer my suggestions and help. Those requests have been ignored.
>
> Since you became Chairman of AIG, you and the Board have presided over the virtual destruction of shareholder value built up over 35 years. It is not my intention to try to point fingers or be critical. My only point is that under the

circumstances, I am truly bewildered at the unwillingness of
you and the Board to accept my help.

Hank

"He just wants to help," Boies said. "He's trying to salvage the company he built." He shook his head with disgust. "One would think," he said, "given his shareholdings, the company would want to talk to him."

I had to agree that it made sense for AIG to consult with him. This was crisis time, and not only did Greenberg hold substantial stock in AIG, he built this company, he knew where the bodies were buried, and he remained close to a number of investors who were of like mind. When I reached Greenberg himself for comment, he told me that he and a group of investors were interested in working with AIG and the Feds on a solution that didn't involve such a big infusion of money. "I would ask for less than $85 billion," he said. "I'd sell assets, do other things to reduce the amount." He told me he had ideas and was willing to serve. But no one was calling.

Greenberg later told me that he would have done everything he could—including perhaps tapping his connections in China and elsewhere—to keep the government out of AIG. And he was suspicious of the terms, which called for the government to pay 100 cents on the dollar to AIG counterparties, chief among them Goldman Sachs. He fumed that the bailout seemed to have as much to do with saving Goldman Sachs as with saving AIG and "the system."

In Washington, Paulson was busy explaining to a nervous White House why the bailout was necessary and why AIG was being saved when Lehman had been allowed to wither. "There is a difference between a capital problem and a liquidity problem," Paulson said, noting that AIG had subsidiaries that could be sold to raise capital. The problem was, once the word was out that AIG was in desperate need of cash, the values on those subsidiaries would begin to drop, and it would be tough to raise the money expected.

By Wednesday the deal was all but done. The government would bail out AIG for $85 billion and assume an 80 percent ownership in the company. (Ultimately, the government would shovel $182 billion into AIG.) In effect, the government now owned AIG. Willumstad would be replaced by Ed Liddy, the retired CEO of Allstate, for the yearly cash compensation of one dollar.

I spoke with Liddy immediately after the announcement. "I feel energized," he said. "I think I can help. I'd like to help this company. I think I can help the country." He seemed deeply sincere and committed to the task.

"But how did this happen?" I asked. "Can you explain how the largest insurance company in the world was actually exploring bankruptcy last weekend?"

"There's a lot of glory to go around," Liddy joked, then turned serious. "Insurance is the oxygen of free enterprise. Nothing can happen without insurance. AIG is interconnected. It touches too many other institutions. Some of the largest banks in the world are carrying credit default swaps, and AIG is insuring them." Reflecting on the image of oxygen, I hoped that AIG and the rest of the financial system would soon be taking large, healthy breaths of air. But realistically, the life support would have to continue for some time.

Dick Fuld was shattered. He had vowed to fight for Lehman until his dying day, and he had lost. It felt like death. In the days and weeks ahead, he would play the events over and over again in his mind, trying to think of a way Lehman's collapse could have been avoided.

"Dick and I had this conversation several times," one of his former colleagues at Lehman told me. "We asked each other what we could have done differently. And we'd say, maybe we should have had a better government relationship, because our interface was woefully inadequate compared with Goldman Sachs and Morgan Stanley. Or we'd say, maybe we shouldn't have had so many illiquid securities. Maybe we should have allocated our capital differently, so we didn't have a high margin business. But then we'd be the laggard in terms of return on equity. The market would have punished us as an underperformer. We kept concluding that it was an industry issue. Look, there were countless things that could have been done that would have saved the day. Like turning into a bank holding company. [Ironically, it wasn't until after Lehman failed that the government allowed the remaining investment banks, Goldman Sachs and Morgan Stanley, the option of becoming bank holding companies.] Like getting a guarantee on the debt Friday night. Like getting a Bank of America or a Barclays deal done. We knew all of the options going in. It wasn't as if we took a left when we should have taken a right."

Characteristically, Fuld remained out of the spotlight, refusing to give interviews or even produce an official statement. Few people would hear from him until October 7, when he sat alone in front of the House Committee on Oversight and Government Reform. The congressmen were angry, looking for answers—and for blood.

Glaring down at Fuld, his dark eyes beneath heavy glasses flashing with outrage, committee chairman Henry Waxman demanded to know why Lehman failed.

Fuld's voice was thick with emotion, and he frequently stumbled over his words. "I do not know why we were the only one . . . I must tell you . . . we walked into that weekend firmly believing that we were going to do a transaction. My employees, my shareholders, my clients, have taken a huge amount of pain." He gazed back at the committee, looking wounded. "Not that anybody on this committee cares about this, but I wake up every single night thinking, 'What could I have done differently? What could I have said? What should I have done?' And I have searched myself every single night. And I come back to this: at the time I made those decisions, I made those decisions with the information I had. I can look at you and say, this is a pain that will stay with me the rest of my life, regardless of what comes out of this committee, and regardless of what the record book will say when it's finally written."

Waxman was not impressed. With a mix of anger and sarcasm, he replied, "I accept the fact that you are still haunted by whether this could have had a different ending. But the system you lived under gave you a very, very generous reward when everything was going up . . . but when things weren't holding up, you still got substantial compensation. We thought you made $500 million; you say that you made only $350 million. That seems to me an incredible amount of money. . . . What I didn't hear from you, Mr. Fuld, is that you say you wished you had done some things differently, but you don't seem to acknowledge that you did anything wrong."

Fuld left the hearings and made his way down the steps of Capitol Hill with his head bowed. A crowd of protesters surrounded him, angry and shouting. One of them shoved a bright pink sign in his face, on which was scrawled a single word: "Crook." It was public anger colliding with free-market capitalism.

SEVEN

Popcorn and Dominoes

"It was extraordinary from a personal point of view. I remember being in the meetings and thinking, 'My gosh, I'm a mere mortal and I'm in a situation where me and half a dozen people hold the fate of three hundred million people in our hands.'"
—ED LAZEAR, ECONOMIST AND CHIEF ECONOMIC ADVISER TO
PRESIDENT GEORGE W. BUSH, IN AN INTERVIEW WITH MARIA
BARTIROMO, FEBRUARY 25, 2010

SEPTEMBER 21, 2008

The mild Sunday evening provided perfect baseball weather, but for the crowds that jammed Yankee Stadium in the Bronx, the victory over the Baltimore Orioles was bittersweet. After eighty-five years and twenty-six world championships, it was the last game to be played at the stadium Ruth built. Twelve miles away, in the caverns of Wall Street, it would also go down as the last day of investment banking as we knew it.

It had been a bad week on Wall Street. Morgan Stanley CEO John Mack, who had watched the disastrous events unfold over the Lehman weekend, and had seen Merrill Lynch jump the investment banking ship to save its life, was deeply troubled. It was becoming increasingly clear that the two remaining investment banks, Morgan Stanley and Goldman Sachs, were vulnerable to the same forces that brought the other three to their knees. Mack knew he had to move fast to save his firm. "It wasn't a question of being scared," he told me. "It was a question of how we were going to solve these problems. After Merrill was bought, Morgan Stanley's and Goldman's stock went down. There was a lot of fear in the market about these firms." Mack started reaching out to international companies that might be investment partners—in particular, Mitsubishi and CIC in China. It was a frustrating period. "What do we have to do to get people to have confidence not only in us but in the entire system? That kind of leadership was the critical piece in keeping the meltdown from being much worse."

The greatest fear during that time was that there would be a run on the investment banks triggered by rumors. True or not, fear would set in and cause people to run for cover and withdraw their money. There was also worry about short-sellers. The concern was so serious that Andrew Cuomo, New York's attorney general, announced that he was launching an investigation into short-sellers. "Short-selling in and of itself is not illegal," he explained to me, "and many people argue that it's a productive part of the marketplace. There can be behavior that is illegal, however, if you've spread false information and are trying to drive down prices for your own economic benefit." A type of short-selling, called naked short-selling, was being investigated by the SEC, and Cox announced a temporary ban on this practice.

Still, Morgan Stanley's stock fell precipitously. In a single week after Lehman declared bankruptcy, the stock price dropped from the low thirties to the low teens. Mack had predicted a "run" on his bank, and now it was happening. In a memo to employees, he warned them to beware of short-sellers and to hold steady in a market controlled by fear and rumors.

During the week he called me to share his frustration. "Maria, when people turn on CNBC and see the headline scrolling across the screen, 'Will Morgan Stanley make it?' what do you think that does to us?" A normally calm guy, Mack was edgy and on the verge of anger.

Mack was constantly on the phone with Paulson and Geithner, as well as with Blankfein. The experience was one of humility, of recognizing that there were no real gods of finance. Everyone was vulnerable. It was one thing to point fingers at individual companies and say, "You did a bad job and you're paying the price." It was quite another to watch stable companies experiencing the aftershocks. There was no time for blame or regrets—only action.

"I don't know if I got four or five calls a day from Hank Paulson, or ten calls," Mack told me, "but he called me a number of times every day, as did Tim Geithner." As the weekend neared, those calls took on greater urgency.

"What is plan B?" Geithner asked Mack. "You've got to find a partner."

Mack and his people were working overtime to do just that. They were talking to the Chinese, to the Japanese, to Warren Buffett. They were talking to Pandit at Citigroup and Dimon at JPMorgan. As they headed into another weekend of all-nighters, Mack was running out of time.

Paulson called Saturday morning. "John," he said, "we cannot have Monday morning open without a solution. It's not just about Morgan Stanley; it's about a financial meltdown on a global basis."

Mack assured Paulson that he understood and that he was in serious discussions with the Japanese about a sizeable investment in Morgan. He and his team spent another night at Morgan Stanley's midtown office.

Sunday morning Mack received a call from the big guns: Paulson, Geithner, and Bernanke. "We see things you don't see," Bernanke said. "This is much bigger than one firm."

"What are you trying to say?" Mack asked cautiously.

"Call Jamie," Geithner said. "He'll buy your bank."

"I've called Jamie. He doesn't want it," Mack replied.

"He wants it now," Geithner said testily. "Call him. He'll buy it."

Mack was running out of patience. "Yeah, he'll buy it for a dollar," he said heatedly. Then he took a deep breath and made his voice very calm. "I have the utmost respect for the three of you," he said. "What you do for this country makes you patriots. But I won't do it." And he put down the phone.

At Goldman Sachs, Blankfein was worried, although the wolves were not yet at his door. He'd told Mack earlier in the week, "You've got to hold on. I'm twenty seconds behind you." He floated the idea to Mack, "Do you think if we were bank holding companies it would help us?" In the end, it turned out to be the solution Mack was looking for, and a way to stop the bleeding that Blankfein knew would ultimately bring him down as well.

On September 21, a mere week after Lehman's fall, a new announcement shook the financial world. The last remaining investment banks, Goldman Sachs and Morgan Stanley, were changing their status to become bank holding companies. On the downside, they would be more strictly regulated, but on the upside they would have access to credit from the Federal Reserve Bank, along with consumer deposits to boost their capital balances.

It was the end of investment banking as it had operated. Goldman Sachs and Morgan Stanley were now more like conventional banks, limited in their ability to make high-risk (and highly lucrative) deals. They were humbled and brought to their knees. Just imagine: in March 2008 there were five great investment banks. Six months later there were none.

Mack wanted to get Morgan Stanley back to basics. He felt that the boom years had led to a loss of discipline in his firm and others. He told me that in the midst of the giddiness of success, "You need to have the discipline to look inward and ask whether this fits with our balance sheet, our capital, and our risk management. Are we stepping out of our comfort zone in investing and trading? The leadership needs to have the discipline to forego the business in the interests of stability—to say, 'I know we may not be as profitable as some of our competitors, but we have a strategy and we're going to stick with that strategy.'"

———

In the Roosevelt Room, a windowless workroom in the West Wing of the White House, dominated by a long, sleek table and high-back chairs, President George W. Bush sat with his top economic team and listened to the bad news. Paulson, Bernanke, and the president's economic advisers sat around the table, taking turns explaining what was happening and offering recommendations. A sense of looming catastrophe was in the air, and it took a great deal of discipline to stay focused.

"I'll tell you, the calmest person in the room was always the president," one of the men in the meetings told me. In spite of the public perception that everyone's hair was on fire in the days following Lehman's collapse, that is not the picture he and others presented of that early period after the weekend that would change Wall Street. "Hank could be an excitable guy, and he wasn't the only one, but the president kept trying to impress on us that we had to keep it on an even keel, think things through, not pull the trigger before we'd taken careful aim. It was an important message, because everything was happening so fast. The president's attitude helped avoid a panic mode.

"This was not like the television show *The West Wing*," he added, "where people are running through the corridors and yelling a lot. We didn't yell. The meetings were very calm, very respectful. I can't remember one meeting ever, even in the height of the crisis when it was very emotional, when there were shouting matches.

"Of course we were nervous. We literally thought we were on the verge of the Great Depression. But never, never in those meetings did you ever see emotion or anger or hysteria. Just didn't happen. I think President Bush did a good job of keeping us steady, and saying, 'Look, you guys, I want you to think this through, and before we do anything, you're going to tell me what you're doing and what it is you think we should be doing, and I want to hear the rationale.'"

One person in the room during many of these critical meetings was Ed Lazear, the president's chief economic adviser. I asked him to give me a sense of what it was like during those days. "There was no average day," he said. "We never knew what each day would bring. The volatility in the system was enormous—especially the market swings. It wasn't crazy to have a five-hundred-point day, and there were even a couple of seven-hundred-point days. I knew when I woke up that every day was going to be at a minimum weird, and at a maximum horrible. What it wouldn't be was a great day."

Lazear's mornings started around 5:15, and while he was still in bed he'd click on CNBC to see what was happening in the international markets. He'd sit in bed and start scribbling notes on the pad he kept on his nightstand. By 6:45 a.m. he was at the office briefing his colleagues and senior staff and making a plan for the day. "We always had a plan," he told me, "even though we had no idea what new crises we'd have to face. We all agreed that we had to take whatever action was necessary to make sure that the market had confidence and that we could ensure that the firms that were so essential to credit and economic growth would survive."

Lazear, an intense guy with a lively face and a shiny bald head, had been plucked from academia to serve the president. He was known as a brilliant economist and an unconventional thinker. When it came to the current financial crisis, he had a theory that was quite unique. He called it the popcorn theory, and he later explained it to me this way: "There were two ways of looking at the crisis. One was the domino view—and it was the most common. Everyone knows the domino theory. One domino topples, it knocks over the next one, knocks over the next one, and the whole thing crashes. Most people thought that was what was going on, and I even thought it myself for a while. When we were back trying to figure out how to prop up Bear Stearns, we actually thought if we kept that domino standing, others wouldn't fall.

"But by May of 2008, I had switched my view to what I call the popcorn theory. Here's how it works. When you're making popcorn, you pour oil in the pan, add the kernels, and then, as the oil gets hot, the kernels start to pop. Now, suppose you take the first kernel out of the pan. It would not stop the other kernels from popping, because the oil is hot. They're going to keep popping as long as the fire is going. Apply this theory to Lehman Brothers. We were all in favor of trying to save Lehman, but even if we'd succeeded, other kernels would keep popping—AIG, Washington Mutual, Wachovia, and so on. I'm not sure it would have prevented stock market damage because it wasn't just Lehman; it was panic in the entire financial system. There was a fundamental problem in the system, and what you had to do was turn the heat off. Or alternatively, you could strengthen the pan—essentially capitalize the financial sector—to withstand all the popping going on inside."

That, according to Lazear, was the reasoning behind the Troubled Asset Relief Program (TARP), an unprecedented effort to turn down the heat on a systemic crisis. "AIG was a big deal, but remember, there were lots of big deals going on right then," Lazear recalled. "Merrill was a big deal; Lehman was a big deal; Fannie and Freddie were a big deal; AIG was a big deal; Washington Mutual and Wachovia were big deals. We had a lot of stuff on our plate at that point, and initially the strategy was to take them one at a time and try to deal with them and prevent any one of them from causing a collapse of the system. But we realized that the piecemeal approach was not an effective strategy.

"I'm an academic by training," he said, "and the historical precedent for this was absent. We'd never seen anything like it. Even in the Great Depression, which people always refer back to, the parallels weren't the same. The Great Depression, in many respects, was worse, but it was worse because it was prolonged. It wasn't worse because of the one initial event. The stock market crash was terrible, but the stuff that happened in those weeks in September 2008 was terrible as well. This was a pretty scary event."

Back in New York, on the floor of the Stock Exchange, I was hearing a lot of frustration over the piecemeal solutions. People were ready for a comprehensive answer. They didn't want to sit there week after week and watch the next bank fail, and the next bank fail. Everyone was looking to Washington to show leadership.

"Even though we said we needed an overall strategy, the truth is, we were not of one mind on what that overall strategy should be," Lazear acknowledged. "It took some time for that to evolve. In retrospect, it would have been better if we'd handled it in a smoother fashion, but it was a war, and like all wars, things don't always go exactly as you plan them. There was an enemy out there. In the end, fortunately, we got it right, and I think TARP was an important component in getting things back on track."

There was no real controversy about TARP at the White House, but the prospect of TARP kicked up some dust on the campaign trail. The administration tried not to be distracted by the presidential race, but there was some concern that politics would sideline their efforts. When McCain appeared on the *Today* show, taking an antibailout position, Paulson got on the phone and talked him down. Barack Obama was more publicly supportive of Paulson's efforts, but there was still a lot of confusion in the country about the meaning and necessity of TARP. The first time it came up for a vote in Congress, it fell short.

"I remember having a meeting with the president right after it failed," a White House source told me. "We all got together in the Roosevelt Room, and the president said, 'Look, we've got to take another shot at it. We can't have this happen. We got to go for it.' So that was the week where we worked the stuff out."

The president's economic team fought back hard against the skeptics. They believed it was time to take a bold chance, and they knew that if they didn't do it, they might end up regretting it later. "It might have been unnecessary," Lazear said with the benefit of hindsight, "but we'll never know. In my view, it was necessary, and it didn't cost the taxpayers very much. Most of the money was repaid. Meanwhile, it was extremely important to get capital into the financial sector to make sure that the pan was strong enough to withstand all the popping going on inside."

The pushback from some free-market capitalists was essentially this: if you believe in free markets, companies should be able to thrive and fail as a result of their own actions. If a firm takes on too much debt and is on its knees, it is appropriate for that firm to go down, with the assets being acquired by another firm. The difference here was that so many firms—AIG in particular—were not so much too *big* to fail as they were too connected to fail. White House economic adviser Keith Hennessey told me that the "intent was to get at the root of the problem. The president's instinct was not to intervene in the markets unless it was absolutely necessary." But the opinion was growing that it was, indeed, just that.

Testifying before the House Financial Services Committee, Paulson stressed that it was essential that the federal government have the power to intervene to save the nation from financial collapse. He added that it was not just a national issue anymore; it was global. In a two-day period at the end of September, the governments of Ireland, the UK, Belgium, France, and Iceland were forced to step in and prevent the failure of financial institutions.

Even with the government plan, Ken Rogoff, the Thomas D. Cabot Professor of Public Policy and professor of economics at Harvard University, predicted many bank failures. "Unless the Treasury decides to buy out every bank, we're going to see more consolidation," he told me on *Closing Bell*. "The industry is coming from a very bloated place—not just bad debt, but the business model itself. I anticipate we'll change the whole way of doing business."

The well-respected economist and author Amar Bhidé also thought TARP was a terrible idea. "I have enormous confidence in the institutions of America," he told me, "and I hope they will override the mistakes individuals make. But this whole business of TARP reminds me a lot of the WMD business in Iraq: 'Oh my God, just trust us. There are these WMDs, and unless you give us the authority now and right now to bomb them, disaster will befall us all.' Giving Wall Street or Detroit or the banks money with virtually no personal accountability erodes the legitimacy of the system. Ultimately, the great strength of this economy is the belief that the game is not rigged, that we can all get ahead if only we try harder. The destruction of that belief could be an awful consequence of this desperate shoveling of money."

There was tremendous relief at the Treasury Department and the White House when TARP passed on October 3, and the government immediately injected $250 billion into the system to stabilize banks. But the relief was extremely short lived. One White House official shuddered recalling what happened next. "After TARP passed, the market fell five hundred points in an hour—which was totally bizarre because this was supposed to be good news. When that happened it was the closest we came to—not panic, but feeling the situation was quite desperate."

In the blame game, one factor kept coming up over and over again—the repeal of the Glass-Steagall Act, a major move toward bank deregulation. Glass-Steagall—named for the two men who wrote the bill, Senator Cantor Glass, Democrat of Virginia, and Representative Henry Bascom Steagall, Democrat of Alabama—became law in 1933, during the height of the Great Depression. At the time there was a strong belief that the collapse of Wall Street was largely due to reckless investing by commercial banks. Glass-Steagall created a barrier between investment and commercial banks that would make such recklessness impossible. However, the law was viewed as a thorn in the side of banking, and the industry had been lobbying for its repeal for many years. Finally, in 1999, the campaign, spearheaded by Senator Phil Gramm of Texas, was successful, and Congress repealed Glass-Steagall. Gramm's efforts had the full support of Federal Reserve chairman Alan Greenspan, Treasury secretary Robert Rubin, and President Bill Clinton. Indeed, Rubin told Congress as early as 1995, "The banking industry is fundamentally different from what it was two decades ago—let alone in 1933." Rubin believed that the rise of globalization demanded a more open and flexible investing environment, and he viewed Glass-Steagall as a roadblock. Later, when Larry Summers replaced Rubin at Treasury in the final years of the Clinton administration, he got on board as well. Many Monday-morning quarterbacks blamed the events of 2008 on this critical piece of deregulation—something I asked Clinton about the week after Lehman's failure. Clinton vehemently denied that the repeal of Glass-Steagall was to blame for Wall Street's collapse, and he defended his administration's decision to repeal the act. "We still have heavy regulations and insurance on bank deposits, requirements on banks for capital and for disclosure," he said. "I thought at the time that repealing Glass-Steagall might lead to more stable investments and a reduced pressure on Wall Street to produce quarterly profits that were always bigger than the previous quarter. But I have really thought about this a lot. I don't see that signing that bill had anything to do with the current crisis."

I pushed him. "Phil Gramm, who was then the head of the Senate Banking Committee, and until recently a close economic adviser of Senator McCain's, was a fierce proponent of banking deregulation. Did he sell you a bill of goods?"

Clinton shook his head. "Not on this bill, I don't think he did. On Glass-Steagall, like I said, if you could demonstrate to me that it was a mistake, I'd be glad to look at the evidence. This wasn't something they [Republicans] forced me into. I really believed that given the level of oversight of banks and their ability to have more patient capital, if you made it possible for commercial banks to go into the investment banking business as Continental European investment banks could always do, that it might give us a more stable source of long-term investment."

Back in the 1990s, the most fervent champion of the repeal of Glass-Steagall was Jamie Dimon's old boss, Sandy Weill. It's likely that only a guy like Weill, with such a remarkable storehouse of grit, and such a giant ego, could have made the impact he did.

In 1996 Weill, then the head of Travelers Insurance, proposed an unprecedented merger of Travelers and Citibank. Such a consolidation was not legal under Glass-Steagall. Weill, along with Citibank head John Reed, and with the tacit backing of Fed chairman Greenspan, began an aggressive campaign against Glass-Steagall that led to its repeal. He was shouting, in effect, "Mr. Clinton, tear down that wall!" The relentless assault on Glass-Steagall finally wore away all resistance in Congress and in the White House. From then on, whenever people talked about the 1999 repeal, Sandy Weill's name was front and center.

Citigroup went on to become a virtual financial superstore—the largest and most complex banking operation in the world. Few could argue with Weill's record of creating a powerhouse in global banking. He was actually ahead of regulation changes, nearly closing the deal with Travelers even before Glass-Steagall ended. But he also stitched together a company rife with conflicts, which created major problems during the peak of the markets when investment bankers were pushing for deals, analysts were recommending their stocks, and everyone was in bed together. It was said at the time that Weill was not above cronyism, such as the time he interceded with the admissions office of the elite 92nd Street Y preschool as a favor to analyst Jack Grubman, who simultaneously upgraded AT&T, later causing regulators to suggest he did it so that Citi could get at AT&T's lucrative investment banking business. This would ultimately help to push Weill out.

When Weill was pressured to step down as CEO in April 2003, he handpicked his lawyer and closest lieutenant, Chuck Prince, as his successor. Although Prince was loyal to Weill and spent seventeen years in his service, he knew nothing about running a global organization with two hundred thousand people. The biggest criticism of Prince among insiders was that he was a lawyer, not a manager. Staffers told me that he rarely listened to advisers, including Weill, and the company faltered severely on his watch. Citigroup stock plummeted from a high of $57 per share to 97 cents during the worst of it. Prince was forced to resign in November 2007, as Citigroup's value plunged. It was clear that Weill's grand vision of a global superstore was being challenged.

With the legacy of Citigroup and other giants of finance and banking in tatters, people were frantically searching for someone to blame. In retrospect, for the broad market, it is clear that the biggest issue was too much easy money. Low interest rates created a very attractive environment to borrow. Too much liquidity had individuals borrowing more and more to buy homes, and Wall Street securitizing those loans to lock in bigger returns.

Greenspan, who had been Fed chairman for seventeen years before stepping down in January 2006, was a target of some who believed that he oversaw an era of irresponsibility that combined low interest rates with too-rapid growth. In late October 2008, he sat before the House Committee on Oversight and Government Reform, looking weary and showing his age.

Henry Waxman, the senior member of the committee, was in a take-no-prisoners mood. "You had the authority to prevent irresponsible lending practices that led to the subprime mortgage crisis," he challenged Greenspan. "You were advised to do so by many others. Do you feel that your ideology pushed you to make decisions that you wish you had not made?"

Greenspan seemed agonized and defeated. "Yes, I found a flaw," he answered honestly. "I don't know how significant or permanent it is, but I've been distressed by that fact." His mea culpa went mostly unappreciated. Congress was out for blood.

The standout image of this period was a line of chief executives— from the banks, the auto companies, and virtually every industry and enterprise—lined up at tables in hearing rooms, ready to take their slaps from Congress. There was plenty of political grandstanding in these hearings, because chief executives were easy targets. The public was expressing outrage, setting its sights on the men and women who had been in charge, and Congress was happy to shift the responsibility.

Humble pie was on the menu during these hearings, and in the middle of the bank crisis, the auto companies showed up wanting help.

"We obviously knew the auto companies were in trouble," a White House official told me. "But what caught us by surprise is how inept they were at taking steps to prevent themselves from going into Chapter 11." Some people in the Bush administration thought that might have been strategic—that the auto companies were holding out for the possibility of an Obama presidency and a friendlier environment. (As president, Obama would propose the banks pay into a fund to pay for their misdeeds but not force the autos to do the same, despite their own poor practices and poor management.)

"Whatever the reasons, they left themselves with no options," a Treasury source said. "They came to us in late October and basically said, 'You've got to give us money or we're going to fail.'" Initially, the administration called their bluff. Instead of giving the auto companies a bailout, they would go to Congress and try to reallocate a $25 billion disbursement for green technology.

It soon became clear that the strategy would not work. The auto companies needed a bailout or they would be out of business by January. "They were helpless because there were no third parties," one observer told me. "There was no Warren Buffett; there was no JPMorgan; there was no one there offering financing for the auto companies."

The fate of America's bedrock enterprises ate up the news cycles during the autumn months. The public was feeling increasingly angry, ripped off, and insecure. As average citizens watched their 401(k)s decline in value, and the worth of their homes plummet, it was natural to villainize the rich Wall Streeters who they perceived had played fast and loose with their money. Much of the public anger was focused on bonuses. Wall Street bonuses, paid in cash and stock options, were legendary. In good times, no one blinked an eye. Face it, when you're making hundreds of millions of dollars for your firm and your investors, who's going to complain? But once TARP and other government bailouts were under way, there was a growing chant that that Wall Street bonuses should be held up or, at the very least, capped. The new administration found a perfect target in the wealthy Wall Streeters who received bonuses. President-elect Obama and his lieutenants fueled the flames of the bonus uproar, and much of the media followed their lead with the simplistic narrative of working-class heroes versus fat-cat villains. Across the land, hardworking people whose compensation was directly tied to their performance, seethed on-air at the sight of executives in failing companies walking away with tens of millions in bonuses. The dispute about executive compensation became a forum for people to express their frustration with the system. In some ways it was a healthy check on the integrity of the financial system and a call to accountability for all business leaders. But in other ways it was an easy scapegoat for the new president to begin an attack on business, which continued well into the midterm election season.

Congress joined the fray. Barney Frank, chairman of the House Financial Services Committee, was angry when he said to me, "These are people who lost enormous amounts of money. How do you give a bonus to someone for having failed so badly, as many of these people did?" (Many people threw back Frank's criticisms, as he had been such a staunch supporter of home ownership for every American, whatever it took, which helped bring about the crisis in the first place.)

At the height of the public outrage over executive compensation and bonuses, things got a little intense. Many Wall Street executives admitted to me that they had hired security companies to protect their families. It was jolting to wake up and find groups of strangers picketing in front of your house. No one doubted that desperation could lead to violence.

In some cases, however, the outrage was unwarranted. I had a source who had worked at AIG, and he got a relatively small bonus of $3,000. But his name was on the bonus list, and so he looked out his window one day and saw picketers and camera crews on his front lawn. He and his family were prisoners in their home for days. He didn't deserve to be made a poster boy for corporate greed, but what happened to him is evidence of the depth of public anger.

Global investor Jim Rogers, who might have had sympathy for the struggling financial institutions, was instead blistering in his contempt. "You know what I would like to see happen?" he said to me. "I'd like to see them let these people go bankrupt, stop bailing them out. There are plenty of banks in America that saw this coming, that kept their powder dry and have been waiting for the opportunity to go in and take over the assets of the incompetent. Likewise, many, many homeowners didn't go out and buy five homes with no income. Many homeowners have been waiting for this, and now all of a sudden the government is saying: 'Well, too bad for you. We don't care if you did it right or not, we're going to bail out the one hundred thousand or two hundred thousand who did it wrong.' I mean, this is outrageous economics, and it's terrible morality."

New York attorney general Cuomo also came out swinging, despite the fact that during the heyday of housing he was running HUD under President Clinton. In that capacity, Cuomo had supported broad home ownership, even though so many people did not have the means to buy homes. Now he was examining whether executives behaved properly, or whether their actions defrauded the public. I asked Cuomo, "Do you worry that politicians and the media have been fanning the flames of class warfare? The bonuses outrage and 'business is bad' theory seem to be obscuring other, perhaps more important, issues, like fixing the financial system and getting credit moving again."

"That is a fair point," he said thoughtfully. "People are rightfully upset about Wall Street abuses and excess. And we need to address those issues. But we also need to be very careful and not let that anger become counterproductive and a distraction. I also think Wall Street should be taking a long, hard look at the philosophy of incentive compensation. I don't think bonuses are always bad. The question for Wall Street is, can it design incentives that promote the long-term health of the firms as opposed to just hitting short-term numbers?"

———

There were so many shock waves in the economy that nobody was wasting energy worrying about the fate of Lehman's doomed executives. Still, it was an extraordinary tale of wealth destruction in a very short period of time. It was a devastating transition for many.

As one executive told me frankly, "In the last twelve months at Lehman, I made $14 million. But $12 million was in stock, and that was completely wiped out. Uncle Sam took a million." He was left with $1 million to pay for a $14 million lifestyle. He had big bank account problems, including a very expensive house to unload. But he smiled and shrugged at his plight.

"Some people are pretty bitter, and they've filed claims and the like," he told me. "My view is that's how it's supposed to work. If the shareholders get wiped out, everyone in the senior managing team should get wiped out. Now, you say, 'Oh, well, this was different.' Screw it. The management team and their interests should be aligned, and, in this case, they were, and they both got wiped out. That's how it worked, and that's how I think it should work."

EIGHT

The Aftershocks

"I don't think we really believed at the time, or understood at the time, just how bad it really was."

—JOHN MACK, CEO OF MORGAN STANLEY, IN AN INTERVIEW WITH
MARIA BARTIROMO, FEBRUARY 13, 2009

In his career, Bob Steel had worked the entire financial circuit—from investment banking (Goldman Sachs) to Treasury to the banking industry (Wachovia), with a couple years' teaching school in between, but in the fall of 2008, he was feeling out of the loop. Steel, fifty-seven years old and North Carolina–raised, had worked for Hank Paulson as under secretary for domestic finance until the summer and now headed up Wachovia Bank. He'd gone in knowing that the bank had issues, but he was confident he could solve them. Now, less than one hundred days later, he was in talks to sell the bank. What a disaster! He would have liked to have discussions with his old colleagues at the Treasury, but it was against the law for him to contact them. He was on his own.

Steel found it hard to resist the metaphor of the raging seas. He told me that prior to the September collapse of Lehman, "It was getting increasingly uncomfortable. And I think that the weaker swimmers, the less strong institutions like Wachovia, found it more and more difficult as the water became choppier and the tide became stronger. It became more and more apparent to us, and to other institutions, that the world was going to be different. We were getting prepared for a period of tumult."

As the fateful weekend in mid-September approached, Steel and his colleagues were already discussing the need to find a strategic investor.

The origins of Wachovia's problems, deeply rooted in the subprime calamity, could be traced to the actions of a husband-and-wife team named Herb and Marion Sandler. At the height of the housing boom, the Sandlers ran a California-based mortgage company called Golden West Financial. Their specialty was option ARMs, loans that featured low teaser interest rates that later ballooned beyond the borrowers' ability to pay. A special invention of the Sandlers' was the "Pick-a-Pay" program. This allowed borrowers to pay low monthly amounts, delaying what they owed by adding to the loan principal. People ended up owing far more than their properties were initially worth.

In their glory days, the Sandlers were praised for their acumen: "Husband, Wife are Golden Duo," raved *Fortune* in 2002. "Golden West Strikes It Gold with Principles," headlined the *Seattle Post Intelligencer* in 2006. That year, Golden West Financial was acquired by Wachovia for $24 billion, and the Sandlers personally made $2 billion on the purchase.

Everyone thought it was a good deal. But at the time it was unknown that Golden West was neck deep in the subprime mess, and the whole thing was about to go under. The golden couple came to be known as "the toxic-mortgage king and queen."

The Sandlers' questionable tactics were outed in the media, including in a scathing feature on *60 Minutes*, but they never took a fall for their business practices. They continued on, donating large sums of money to political candidates (mostly Democrats), funding the investigative journalism outfit ProPublica, and standing on the sidelines when Wachovia started to fail as a result of their actions.

On Friday, September 26, 2008, the run on Wachovia started. Alarm bells were ringing loud in Steel's office. The day before, the FDIC had seized Washington Mutual. Steel was desperate. He had to find a buyer, and he had two potentials: Wells Fargo and Citigroup. On Sunday, Steel had breakfast with Dick Kovacevich, CEO of Wells Fargo, and he briefly thought that Kovacevich was ready to make a firm offer. But it never came. Meanwhile, the Fed was getting into the act, brokering a deal with Citigroup.

For an entire week it appeared that the Citigroup purchase was a done deal—all over but the toasting. Then, on Friday, October 3, Wachovia and Wells Fargo made a joint announcement, stating that Wachovia had accepted a Wells Fargo bid of $15 billion for the bank. Over at Citigroup, no one was amused. In fact, Citi was threatening legal action, saying it had already assumed risk. When I spoke with Steel and Kovacevich later that day, both men shrugged off Citi's claim. "There was no merger agreement," Steel said. I could tell he was delighted to be a part of Wells Fargo. "It's a win-win," he said. "Good for the government—not a penny of government money. Also, we have similar values and ethics, and operate in similar communities."

I was curious about how Wells Fargo managed to rise above

the devastation, and I asked Kovacevich. "We just didn't make some of the mistakes that others did," he said. "We still made some mistakes, and that's very unfortunate. In some cases, we should have known better. In general—and I don't know if I take much pride in this—we're probably the least ugly of the ugly ducks because we did not participate in some of the excesses."

Warren Buffett, Wells Fargo's biggest shareholder, was on CNBC October 3 defending the deal. He was unconcerned about Citigroup's threat of legal action. "I know it's a better deal, obviously, for the Wachovia shareholders," he said. "And I know that there is no company, there's no banking institution, during the last six months, that has done a better job for its holders, for its depositors, and for its borrowers, than Wells. Wells has been lending more and more money. They've been pumping money into the economy during the last six months while other institutions have been contracting. So I think Wells is a wonderful home for Wachovia."

Steel was a happy man. He had weathered the storm. But these were frightening days for the average person. People were asking, "Is my money safe?" This lack of confidence was reflected in the plummeting stock numbers.

"I always ask, what did we do wrong?" a government source told me. "Well, what we did wrong was we should have started capitalizing the financial sector back in March of 2008, maybe even a little bit earlier, to make sure companies had sufficient funds to withstand these liquidity runs. But the problem was we couldn't even get Congress to pass it the first time after the Lehman failure, after the AIG failure, you know, with Wachovia and Washington Mutual, with Fannie and Freddie failing, with the runs on the investment banks. You still couldn't get them to pass it. So there was no chance we could have gotten them to pass it earlier. I think the evidence is clear on that, that you needed some pretty catastrophic events to get this stuff through Congress."

He added that he always got annoyed when people started pointing fingers at the sellers and not the buyers. "Everybody's to blame," he said. "If you were to add up all the blame, it would equal seven hundred percent. But, in my mind, the people who were most problematic were the people who bought these assets and didn't think them through."

———

As 2008 wound to a close, Hank Paulson was in a contemplative mood. He was preparing to leave Washington at the end of the Bush administration and was looking forward to spending more time on his farm in Illinois. He planned to write a book and had been offered a teaching fellowship at Johns Hopkins University. He knew his life would be full. But he also knew that his career would be defined by the events of 2008, and he wasn't shy about defending his decisions and actions during those critical months. We sat down together for one final conversation before Paulson left the Treasury.

"Where are we in terms of recovery?" I asked.

He smiled. "Well, Maria, that's the question everybody is asking." I could see that he wanted to analyze what had been achieved. Paulson had been sitting atop the bucking bronco for nearly a year. He was proud that he'd taken firm control and had not allowed a complete collapse of the system. "We stemmed a string or cycle of financial institution failures, which could have led to a downward spiral—a freefall for the economy," he said, adding that the less sexy, long-term work of stabilization was still ahead.

I looked Paulson in the eye and asked, "Do you regret allowing Lehman to fail?"

He sighed. I imagine he'd been asked that question hundreds of times, and given his decency, he'd probably lost sleep over it. He seemed mildly frustrated to have to go back over it—the fact that pre-TARP, the government had no authority to save Lehman. Although it clearly pained him that a solution had not been found that weekend, he was quietly defiant about the suggestion that he could have done anything differently. However, I noticed that when he left the interview, Paulson did not have the old spring in his step. The crisis had aged him and changed him. He'd be turning over the reins of the Treasury to the man he had worked with so closely, Tim Geithner. But Geithner would be answering to an administration with a different attitude toward Wall Street. Paulson couldn't predict what would happen to his carefully crafted solutions once the Obama team took office.

———

John Thain was having a very, very bad morning on January 22, 2009. Ken Lewis had phoned the day before from Charlotte to schedule an urgent meeting in Thain's New York office for 11:30 a.m. Thain could only guess what Lewis wanted, but the thought of his boss's private plane barreling north was not a comforting one.

It had been four months since the triumphant announcement of Merrill's sale to Bank of America, which had saved the investment firm's hide in the wake of Lehman's failure. Thain had agreed to stay on to support the merger and to ease the way in what would be a complex venture. It was difficult to explain to anxious shareholders that the sale did not mean an overnight correction. Merrill still had problems on the books, although Thain was working overtime to divest the company of the remaining toxic assets. He had anticipated all along that it would be a difficult several months. The deterioration of the market had continued, and though he'd been aggressive in moving away from mortgage-related products, there were still enough of them on the books to cause pain. There were huge spreads between the prices of cash assets and credit default swaps, and any type of forced selling drove asset prices down. That meant more losses before Merrill started to climb back.

Merrill's vulnerabilities should not have been a surprise to Lewis, either. Right after the agreement in September, he'd moved his accountants into the Merrill offices, and they knew about Merrill's problems better than anyone. By the time Bank of America's shareholders formally approved the merger on December 5, Thain felt optimistic that the two companies could successfully move forward. What he didn't fully grasp was the extreme sensitivity involved in combining two cultures—the staid world of commercial banking and the comparatively high-flying world of investment banking. With the official takeover date scheduled for January 1, 2009, Thain was focusing a lot of his energy in December on taking care of his own people—specifically, making sure that $4 billion in bonuses were in place. There were reports that he also requested a bonus of $10 million for himself, stating that he deserved the large sum because he "saved Merrill" with the sale to Bank of America. In doing so he missed the mood of the company—and of the nation. He failed to see that with Merrill still bleeding, the bonuses might have been perceived by Bank of America shareholders and by members of Congress as terribly inappropriate. (It deserves note that to this day Thain denies asking for $10 million, but directors who were there told the media a different story.)

By December Lewis had grown deeply concerned. He later told me, "The losses began to really accelerate in mid- to late December. November was bad, but November was bad for almost every company in the business. And there was a point in mid-December that we said, 'Hey, things are accelerating and we need to call for a material adverse change.'"

A material adverse change (MAC) is a legal contingency clause that allows an acquiring company to halt completion of a transaction if the status of the company it's acquiring changes measurably, and that's what Lewis was seeing.

"We went to the Treasury and the Fed," he told me, "and we talked to them about that. And we jointly concluded that it would pose some systemic risk if the deal didn't go through. They promised to assist us in getting it done and filling the bucket of capital that was taken away by the loss."

"Did they say, 'No, no, no, you can't walk away from it?'" I asked.

"They said, 'We strongly advise you that it is not in your best interest or the country's best interest to walk away from this,'" Lewis explained. "And at the end of the day, we thought it was in our best interest and the country's best interest to go ahead with it, because we still saw the long-term strategic benefits. And we thought the disruption caused by not doing it just outweighed calling the MAC."

The government assist involved the promise of an additional $20 billion in stimulus funds. But Lewis could not contain a sense of doom as the announcement of fourth-quarter losses loomed. There was no way to sugarcoat the news: Bank of America posted a loss by Merrill of more than $15 billion.

Unquestionably, there were those at Bank of America who had the knives out for Thain. The bonus issue was bad enough, but then someone leaked an old story that put Thain in a very bad light. The story involved Thain's start at Merrill Lynch a year earlier, when he had spent more than $1.2 million in the renovation of his office, including $131,000 for area rugs, a $68,000 antique credenza, a $35,000 commode, and a $1,400 wastebasket. This was the type of excess that might have been acceptable in the frothy days just past, but it did not go down well with taxpayers in the throes of recession. Never mind that it had happened a year earlier, before the crisis hit. The media slammed Thain, focusing on the $45 billion in stimulus funds that had landed in Bank of America's coffers. The point got mangled but nobody cared: John Thain was viewed as the guy who spent a small fortune on office commodes and wastebaskets—and then demanded a $10 million bonus while the taxpayers wrote fat checks to his company.

In spite of the bad press, Thain did not feel the personal jeopardy that was looming on January 22. Shortly before noon, Lewis entered his corner office, his demeanor cool and unfriendly. He sat down and got right to the point. "Things aren't working out. We're going to replace you." While Thain was digesting this bitter news, Lewis added that the blame for fourth-quarter losses was going to land squarely in Thain's lap. End of conversation. This wasn't a negotiation; it was a firing. The meeting was over in fifteen minutes.

Thain was shaken to the core. They were only twenty-two days into the merger, and he had agreed to stay because he was convinced he could make a positive difference for the two companies, especially during the transition process. Fourth-quarter results aside, he was already seeing good results in January. He couldn't believe that Lewis was firing him just as they were getting started.

The minute the news broke, I was on the phone trying to reach Thain. I was eager to hear his side of the story. Finally, that weekend, as I was packing to leave for Davos, Switzerland, to cover the World Economic Forum, Thain returned my call. He agreed to do an on-air interview—his first—on Monday.

As my plane crossed the ocean to Switzerland, I thought about the questions I would ask. I vividly recalled the critical weekend in September when the future of the financial system seemed to hang in the balance. I remembered thinking how courageous Thain was that weekend—stepping up and making a bold move to save his company. Was this just a clash of cultures? Was it a warning about the level of toxic assets still buried in the banks? Was it a story about Wall Street not getting it?

"John," I said, at the start of our interview, "Merrill paid out $4 billion in bonuses to Merrill's top players. How can you justify losing $15 billion in a three-month period and still be paying out bonuses at a time when you were forced to sell to a larger player, and you were going to the government for needed capital? How do you justify paying out all of that money?"

His answer was similar to what I had heard many times over from others on Wall Street. "If you don't pay your best people, you will destroy your franchise. Those best people can get jobs other places, and they will leave. So the necessity to maintain the franchise is why you really have to pay some amount of bonuses, because, as you know, Wall Street people's salaries tend to be relatively small.

And their bonuses are the vast majority of their compensation for the year." I knew that many listeners would find the explanation arrogant and tin-eared. Here was a company that had lost more than $15 billion in the fourth quarter, and Thain's defense of bonuses in light of the company's problems would not garner much support from the public.

I also asked Thain about his expensive office renovation. At the very least, this was a public relations problem; at most, it betrayed a gross insensitivity.

"It was an environment where jobs were being cut and salaries were being cut," I said. "And the firm was reporting all of these losses. Did it occur to you at some point over the process to say, 'This is probably not the best judgment. I better put this off'?" I asked.

He began defensively. "Well, first of all, this was a year ago or actually a little bit more than a year ago, in a very different economic environment, and a very different outlook for Merrill and the financial services industry. It was my office. It was two conference rooms and it was a reception area. But it is clear to me in today's world that it was a mistake. I apologize for spending that money on those things. And I will make it right. I will reimburse the company for all of those costs."

I was curious, though, as were many people, about what was so wrong with former Merrill Lynch CEO Stan O'Neal's office that such an expensive renovation would be necessary. His explanation was unconvincing, and he squirmed as he tried to explain that O'Neal's office was outside the standard set by Merrill. "It really would have been very difficult for me to use it in the form that it was in." He seemed to be implying that the place was a dump. Who believed *that*? Actually, I later learned that O'Neal was much more egregious in his office spending, insisting on having clear glass walls and a very modern decor with white and glass everywhere. It seemed to me he'd gotten off easy, considering the level of debt and lavish spending on his watch.

Thain was clearly embarrassed by the situation. "With twenty-twenty hindsight, it was a mistake," he said. "I'm sorry that I did that. And I intend to fully reimburse the company."

But it was too late for Thain to fully make amends. The story would tarnish him, although he would reemerge before long as the CEO of troubled lender CIT Group.

I was also curious about Ken Lewis's role in a deal that was looking more problematic by the day. Although the sale of Merrill Lynch to Bank of America had been considered good news in the midst of a catastrophic weekend, many people were troubled by the rapidity of the agreement and wondered how Lewis could possibly have done due diligence in the space of forty-eight hours. I also wondered about the personal dynamic between two very strong-willed, ambitious men whose cultural differences ran deep. I'd heard that since the acquisition, Thain avoided Charlotte whenever possible, and the two men spent little time getting their management and future plans in sync. One glaring example: Thain had no idea that Lewis had tried to pull out of the deal on the MAC clause in December.

On February 10, I caught up with Lewis in Washington, D.C., when he joined me for an interview on CNBC. I put it to him bluntly. "Clearly, the losses at Merrill have been stunning: $15 billion in the fourth quarter alone. Once you saw the losses piling up, how did it happen that you went forward? Investors want to know, what were you thinking when you allowed this deal to go through?"

Lewis was uncharacteristically edgy. He reiterated that the Treasury and the Fed urged him to complete the deal, saying, "Too much damage will be done to the industry, to the country, and to you" if the deal didn't go through. "And so it got to be in some ways, enlightened self-interest. Because we're so inextricably tied in with the U.S. economy, and have such large market shares, that what's good for America is good for Bank of America."

"But did you feel strong-armed?" I asked. "Did they say, 'Look, we may take you out of a job'?"

"I promise you, that was not a factor," he said firmly. "This was about their advice. And then, as we reflected on it, we agreed it was the right thing to do."

And why, I wondered, had he fired Thain?

Lewis definitely didn't want to talk about it. "I almost feel like that's ancient history," he said of the firing, which was only three weeks old. He had already moved on and had effectively thrown Thain under the bus.

But Thain's ouster was hardly the end of the story. Bank of America's purchase of Merrill Lynch continued to haunt Lewis. At the end of 2009, Lewis was forced out of Bank of America, a breathtaking fall from grace. Two months later, on February 4, 2010, New York attorney general (and soon-to-be governor of New York) Andrew Cuomo filed fraud charges against him, stating that he had hidden the scope of Merrill's problems. "We believe the bank management understated the Merrill Lynch losses to shareholders," Cuomo said. "Then they overstated their ability to terminate their agreement to secure $20 billion of TARP money, and that is just a fraud. Bank of America and its officials defrauded the government and the taxpayers at a very difficult time. This was an arrogant scheme hatched by the bank's top executives who believed they could play by their own set of rules. In the end, they committed an enormous fraud, and American taxpayers ended up paying billions for Bank of America's misdeeds." Lewis hired attorney Mary Jo White, now a private lawyer whose former job for nine years was as a U.S. attorney for the Southern District of New York, litigating white-collar crime from the other side. White stated, "There is not a shred of objective evidence to support the allegations by the attorney general."

Regardless of the legal outcome, the deal that had so many people praising the team of Lewis and Thain in 2008 had become a giant black mark for both of them. Lewis might well have wondered how it all happened. Hadn't he been the good guy, the dignified Southern banker who eschewed Wall Street's culture of greed? Hadn't he rescued Merrill?

Lewis was quickly replaced by Brian Moynihan, the fifty-year-old lawyer who had been serving as Merrill's CEO. I caught up with Moynihan on the Bank of America trading floor, and he cheerfully told me how the transfer of power came down. "I was in Charlotte for other reasons, and they said, 'You need to stay around.' And the board has their meeting and someone came down and said, 'They need you to come upstairs.' I walked in, and the board greeted me with a round of applause, and gave me a hug and said, 'You're the new CEO.' I said that was terrific."

He smiled broadly and I returned it. "That was the easy part," I said. "Now the hard part begins." It was true. With the acquisition fever of recent years, Bank of America had joined Citigroup on the poster for "too big to fail" banks, and that was not a good place to be. The deal that would hurt most—Countrywide Financial.

"Can you categorically say no more acquisitions for the near term?" I asked Moynihan, knowing what his answer would be. With Lewis gone, no one at a bank built on a long string of mergers had much stomach for expansion. Instead, the new ideal was lean and mean. Even worse, the string of foreclosures and mortgages gone bad would haunt Bank of America for years to come.

———

As the months rolled on, many began to talk about the fact that things were not as they had seemed that weekend in September, when the crisis appeared to revolve around the fate of a single investment firm, Lehman Brothers. Truths were revealed in a trickle, not a flood, and everyone was too focused on surviving to contemplate the larger picture.

Back in January, in his final interview with me as Treasury secretary, Hank Paulson had told me during a commercial break, "In six months you will understand why we did what we did." He meant spending upwards of $1 trillion bailing out major banks without revealing which banks got the money. I thought it was a mysterious remark, but the government secrecy finally became clear: it was hiding Citigroup's potential insolvency.

In the wake of the financial crisis, the superstore that was Sandy Weill's brainchild was in real trouble. Vikram Pandit had been CEO for less than a year, but he had to be thinking his ascension came at the worst possible time. Sources told me that the potential failure of Citigroup was of such concern to government officials that they devised the wall of secrecy for all banks, solely to prevent Citigroup's weakness from being revealed. But by November 2008, its problems were too great to hide. The $25 billion TARP contribution did not even begin to cover the bank's asset drain. Was it possible Citigroup could go down? The idea sent a shudder through Wall Street that was felt around the world.

Observing events with special interest was Prince Alwaleed of Saudi Arabia. The nephew of Saudi Arabia's King Abdullah, Alwaleed, fifty, could be something of a loose canon, but he was also Citigroup's largest shareholder. When he first invested in Citigroup, it was seen as a smart move, and his net worth was estimated at more than $21 billion. He was always very opinionated about the company and its management. He loved Weill, and when I spoke to him in 2006, shortly after Weill's retirement from the board, he didn't attempt to hide his displeasure with Citigroup's downward trajectory. He told me of a meeting he'd had with Weill and Chuck Prince in Paris. "We discussed the promise from Chuck that he will deliver good results," Alwaleed told me. "If I can quote him, he said: 'We have put the big problems of Citi behind us.'"

"So, how long a grace period are you giving Chuck Prince?" I asked Alwaleed.

"The grace period is over," he said tightly. "You can quote me on that."

By November 2008, Chuck Prince was long gone, but Alwaleed was still heaping scorn on his tenure. He recounted a meeting with Sandy Weill, which occurred at some unspecified time in the past. "Immediately when he met me he said, 'Prince Alwaleed, I'm sorry,' and I asked him, 'Sorry for what, Sandy?' He said, 'I'm sorry for appointing Chuck Prince.'"

The blame game was on. Alwaleed said, "Frankly speaking, the destruction of all that took place recently, clearly has to be attributed to the previous management. Now it is the Vikram era, and you have to look at the positive side, at what could take place at Citigroup. Open a new page, put the worst behind us."

Of course, that was before the revelations came about Citigroup's troubles, or before Pandit and the Feds began to lock horns. In June 2009 it was reported that Federal Deposit Insurance Corporation chief Sheila Bair was pushing hard for a shake-up at Citi that would include getting rid of Pandit.

I asked Pandit, "How much heat are you feeling, and will you step aside?" He replied in his typically even-mannered way, "Given the losses we've taken, and until we return to sustainable profitability, we will have speculation. That doesn't make the speculation correct." He didn't say so, but by implication Pandit felt that Bair's attacks were unwarranted, in light of his aggressive efforts to streamline the company. "We're a much smaller Citigroup," he said. "More important, we want to be Citicorp, not Citigroup, going forward. Citicorp is our global bank for consumers and businesses. At the same time, we've also decided there are some businesses we need to sell. We closed one of them, the Morgan Stanley Smith Barney joint venture. And we're methodically selling and rationalizing what we call Citi Holdings."

Bair was unsuccessful in forcing an ouster of Pandit; there was an almost deadening silence around her charges. No one else seemed willing to step up and call for Pandit to go. Indeed, many people believed that it was wrong to blame Pandit, a relatively recent arrival, for Citi's problems. And he seemed to be taking action to make the company more manageable. In fact, Pandit would end up cutting $500 billion from the balance sheet by selling assets and very methodically raising cash.

Citi was saved, for the time being, but it was still limping along. Amid $45 billion in bailouts and Pandit's streamlining campaign, Sandy Weill was in the background, trying to get involved—maybe even to come back, although that seemed like wishful thinking on the part of people like Prince Alwaleed and Weill himself. Like Hank Greenberg with AIG, Weill might have thought he could play a role, but his efforts to insinuate himself were rebuffed—as were Greenberg's. These old fighters, who, one must not forget, were the architects and engineers of enormous global enterprises, could not let go.

Jim Rogers did not feel much pity for the perpetrators when he talked to me about the collapse of integrity within the system. "They all took huge, huge profits," he railed. "Who was the head of Citigroup? Chuck Prince? I mean, how many hundreds of millions of dollars did Prince take out of the company? How many hundreds of millions of dollars did other Citibank execs take out of the company? Wall Street has paid something like $40 billion or $50 billion in bonuses in the past decade. Look at Stan O'Neal at Merrill Lynch. He got $150 million for leaving, even though he ruined the company. Look at the guy at Fannie Mae, Franklin Raines. He did worse accounting than Enron. Fannie Mae and Freddie Mac alone did nothing but pure fraudulent accounting year after year, and yet that guy's walking around with millions of dollars. What the hell kind of system is this?"

———

A year after the weekend that changed Wall Street, I broadcast a special on CNBC, called *One Year Later: Reflections from the Street*.

Along with my producers at CNBC, I gathered some of the primary players from that weekend—all older, wiser, and perhaps sobered by the wild run that nearly destroyed our financial system.

"There's a calmness back in the market," John Mack told me, "although people are still shell-shocked. Everyone has gone out of their way—including we at Morgan Stanley—to make sure that we're in a better position as we go forward in these markets, meaning we've raised a lot of capital. We have a new regulator in the Federal Reserve as a bank holding company. That's a big change from where we were a year ago. It's huge. And, of course, we've looked at our risk management—where did we make mistakes, where do we need to add more resources? So, one year later everyone is feeling better, but everyone is still concerned."

This response—relief on one hand, concern on the other—was reflected in the comments of nearly everyone I spoke to during that period. But the attitude was like that of a patient who was on life support a week ago being upgraded to critical. He's not dying anymore but he's still very, very sick.

"It has been like a slow-moving cardiac arrest," Mohamed El-Erian observed. "As opposed to a sudden stop, you've had a number of smaller stops in the system. And we kept the patient, which is the financial system, alive in the ICU, using a tremendous amount of medication. And the patient is better, but he's still in the hospital and he's still dependent on medication. But there's an understanding that over time the medication needs to be reduced and eventually even stopped. But there's also an understanding that unless the patient changes his behaviors, he'll end up back in the hospital."

Perhaps the patient would like to change his behavior, perhaps not. But it will certainly be hard to do while the fallout from early crises keep invading his well-being. I have always known that it would take years, and maybe even decades, before we fully understood all the factors behind the near collapse of our financial system in 2008.

———

When your public and professional actions cause the spotlight to be extended to your family, it's extremely rough. It is in many cases sad and unfair. Lehman executives, along with many others in the financial industry, found their private lives put on display. The narrative was irresistible: financial fat cats living large while Middle America loses its pension benefits. For a time the cameras were out in force, trolling the wealthy communities of Greenwich, Connecticut; Harrison, New York; and other enclaves of privilege.

Former Lehman trader Larry McDonald, for one, spared no sympathy for the Fulds. "Dick Fuld should publicly apologize," he told me. "So many people are in pain. Their unemployment has run out, their COBRA [health insurance] has run out. These are back-office people."

It is impossible to calculate the scope of the suffering in Middle America that resulted from the crisis, but just among the doomed employees of Lehman Brothers and other failed banks, the pain rose to an intolerable level.

Meanwhile, umbrellas, ties, duffel bags, coffee cups, and other items bearing the Lehman Brothers logo started making an appearance on eBay. The sales would go toward paying Lehman's creditors.

Months later, long after Lehman Brothers had disappeared from the front pages and faded from public interest, the court-appointed examiner who had been quietly studying the events leading up to Lehman's bankruptcy filed a 2,200-page report. Suddenly, Lehman was back in the spotlight. I suppose the good news, if you were Fuld or Gregory or Callan or anyone else in a critical position, was that there didn't appear to be criminal charges in the offing—at least, not yet. But that didn't mean there wouldn't be lawsuits and legal challenges, because the report made a strong case that Lehman was hiding the truth in the months before it fell.

Deserving particular scrutiny was its use of a device called Repo 105 in the second quarter of 2008 to move $50 billion off its balance sheet. A repo is a sales and repurchasing agreement that involves transferring assets in exchange for cash, with an agreement to repay the money and take back the assets later. In principle, it's not much different than a loan, where assets are held as collateral on future payment. The difference in Repo 105 was that Lehman recorded it as a sale and no longer had any record of the assets on its balance sheet. Nor did the firm disclose Repo 105.

In a daylong hearing before the House Financial Services Committee on April 20, characterized as an "autopsy" of Lehman, Fuld insisted that he was completely unaware of Repo 105. "I have absolutely no recollection whatsoever of seeing documents related to Repo 105 transactions while I was the CEO of Lehman," he said. Was he credible?

Such fancy footwork certainly breaks the spirit, if not the letter, of the law. Mary Schapiro, who replaced Christopher Cox as head of the SEC, admitted to Congress that the agency's oversight was sorely lacking—right up to the moment of Lehman's bankruptcy. Its investigators only skimmed the surface, looking at obvious trades and statements. They didn't go deep enough to uncover Repo 105.

When I caught up with Schapiro in Washington on March 29, 2010, she told me that not only was the SEC looking very carefully at Lehman, but it was examining every major financial institution to see if there were "Repo 105–type issues." Schapiro was a fresh face and offered new hope that the SEC would no longer be asleep at the wheel. She inspired some confidence in regulatory circles. Even before the latest Lehman revelations, many people had viewed Cox's tenure as lax, exemplified by Bernie Madoff's $65 billion swindle, which happened right under the agency's eyes. There was also an odd item breaking about SEC investigators watching pornography on their office computers at the height of the crisis. One staffer had watched porn for eight hours straight! Could it get any worse?

When the SEC does not perform its role, and institutions get away with deceptive practices and worse, it tarnishes the credibility of the financial system. This is not just a symbolic black mark. The markets rely on investor confidence, and when that is shaken the results are recorded in tangible declines on balance sheets. Just consider how many millions of people pulled their money out of the stock market between September and December 2008. Their actions were fear driven and may have gone against the best advice of their financial advisers, but it didn't matter. Once confidence was gone, the stock market couldn't operate effectively. But one Bush administration source noted to me that "the market is a tough taskmaster and it punishes bad behavior pretty harshly. I don't think we will ever have a repeat of the kind of crisis that we had in the past."

It was a good start. But as the revelations kept coming, and Americans kept bearing the burden, many of them wanted to see bankers going to the woodshed. Tactically, the financial-reform discussions centered on the boogeyman dubbed "too big to fail."

The scares surrounding the potential collapse of institutions like AIG and Citigroup opened a debate about whether any institution should be allowed to grow to the extent that its collapse put the nation—or the global economy, for that matter—in jeopardy. New regulations would become the next change that was to be met on Wall Street. Under the aegis of the Dodd Amendment, sponsored by Senator Chris Dodd of Connecticut, the Senate introduced a wind-down amendment that allowed regulators to break up banks whose failure could pose a "grave threat" to the financial system.

On two occasions in the space of months I interviewed Treasury secretary Geithner about the government's response to "too big to fail." He told me that they had been working hard to find the right way to stop a crisis before it spread. "The key point is, that if big banks ever manage themselves to the edge that they cannot survive without government assistance," he said, "the government should have the ability to come in and dismember them and unwind them and sell them off in pieces without putting the taxpayers at risk. We don't want the taxpayers to be at exposure of nearing the costs of the large financial crisis.

"One way to think about it is to use the firefighting metaphor," he added. "You want to draw a fire break around the fire, and make sure that the fire can't jump from the failing firm and threaten the rest of the financial system." It seemed self-evident to me—so obvious, in fact, that I marveled that such a plan had not been in place at the time of the financial collapse around Lehman. Geithner agreed. "A tragic failure of the country," he said, nodding vigorously. "We had it in place for small banks, but we didn't have it in place for large, complex institutions that dominated the world—for Fannie and Freddie, and AIG, and Lehman, and Bear Stearns, and even the major banks in the country. The only authority the president had was to come in and shut down the markets and declare a bank holiday."

Geithner and I discussed the matter at some length. I didn't question his sincerity, or even his incredibly bright mind, which was on full display when he relaxed and opened up one-on-one. At the time of our last interview, in the early spring of 2010, I noted that he looked older and more burdened than he had in September 2008—and no wonder.

"We are not going back to the system the way it was," he said firmly, but the new direction was less clear. He spoke of fundamental change, but he couldn't explain exactly what that would mean.

NINE

A Greek Tragedy

"Our debt is $13 trillion. To give you an idea of what a trillion is, if the day that Jesus Christ was born somebody put a million dollars into a bank account and then added another million dollars every single day for the next two thousand and ten years, you still wouldn't have a trillion."

—DAVID RUBENSTEIN, COFOUNDER AND MANAGING DIRECTOR OF
THE CARLYLE GROUP, DISCUSSING THE ENORMITY OF OUR DEBT IN
MY PANEL DISCUSSION AT THE ASPEN IDEAS FESTIVAL, JULY 9, 2010

SPRING 2010

In a classic Greek tragedy, the protagonist suffers a fall as a result of a fatal flaw. By 2010 this had become an apt metaphor for the sinking fortunes of Greece, which threatened the European Union and the stability of the euro itself. Greece had long been a profligate spender, continuing to pay the bill for an excessive national standard of living, even as it was going broke. Those who might have asked why we should care about what happened to this tiny country across the ocean could find an answer in the dangerous debt load that was building here at home.

Greece mattered because it was emblematic of what sovereign debt (that is, government-owned debt) could do, and as such was a cautionary tale for the bailout-strapped United States. If debt brought about the crisis on Wall Street in 2008, the transformation of private debt to government debt was in many ways the story of the post–September 2008 economy.

By the time 2010 came around, there was a sense that the panic was dying down, and we were headed toward daylight, even if we were not there yet. But stability seemed to be coming up against some difficult economic and political realities. The crisis on Wall Street in 2008 and the enormous capital spent on bailouts empowered a new administration to push for more stringent financial regulations. No one knew for sure how strict the regulatory environment would become, but many critics felt that the administration should be more focused on the growing debt. A year and a half after the financial crisis, our debt was more than $14 trillion, larger than the U.S. economy, and it was expected to rise to $16.9 trillion by 2015.

According to the Council on Foreign Relations, foreign ownership of U.S. debt has increased dramatically over the last decade. Foreigners now hold 57 percent of U.S. Treasuries, while foreign holdings of U.S. government agency and government-sponsored-entity debt have increased from 6 to 16 percent. Virtually the entire increase in both has been accounted for by foreign governments, as opposed to private investors. And one government dominates: China. According to the *Wall Street Journal*, China has accumulated an astounding $850 billion in Treasuries and $430 billion in agency debt over the last decade—almost half the total foreign government accumulation.

Former Treasury secretary Hank Paulson revealed in his book, *On the Brink*, that in August 2008 he learned that "Russian officials had [earlier] made a top-level approach to the Chinese suggesting that together they might sell big chunks of their GSE holdings to force the U.S. to use its emergency authorities to prop up these companies," referring to the debt issued by Fannie Mae and Freddie Mac. Paulson said that the Chinese declined to cooperate but noted that the report was "deeply troubling," as "heavy selling could create a sudden loss of confidence in the GSEs and shake the capital markets." With the United States needing to sell another $1.3 trillion in debt this year, should be we worried about these concerns and should the structure of the GSEs be changed?

Ben Bernanke tried to calm such fears back in 2006. "It would be very much against their own interest to do so," said the Fed chief. "Heavy selling would precipitate precisely the fall in the dollar's local and global purchasing power that the Chinese fear. So the Chinese would not cut off their noses to spite their faces." Still, there is no question that foreign ownership of U.S. debt has put us in a less secure position internationally.

In January, when I was covering the World Economic Forum in Davos, Switzerland, the alarm bells were sounding about sovereign debt. When discussing the next global crisis, Ken Rogoff, a professor of economics at Harvard, gave an impassioned warning. "Government money brought us back," he acknowledged, "but it morphed into a long-term debt crisis—an illusion of normalcy. The crisis is over because governments guaranteed everything and spent like drunken sailors." Rogoff gave the bailout its due, noting that it was a good thing that we didn't have a second Great Depression. "The problem is," he added, "if one looks at history, banking crises are too often followed by a wave of sovereign debt crises a few years later. No surprise, [today] debt is exploding. In countries like the U.S., we may see painful political consequences—belt tightening, higher taxes, slower growth. In emerging Europe, we could see worse, including outright default. We may tell ourselves we're better; we've figured things out; we won't have the political problems other countries have faced; we're different. But I submit to you, we're not."

Not everyone agreed with Rogoff's position, but almost like clockwork, when I arrived back in New York from Davos, the focus turned to Europe and a staggeringly slow recovery. CEOs from Hewlett-Packard to Coach told me Europe was stuck in the mud, unable to break out of the grips of recession. And now the new focus was government debt, particularly in Greece and its impact on the rest of Europe.

Since Greece was part of the eurozone, consisting of sixteen states that use the euro as their sole currency, there was deep concern over the possibility that the entire region could be on the hook to bail them out. Once again, we were dealing with "too big to fail," only this time it was on a national level. How many American companies would be exposed, and how deep would the contagion run? These worries gripped the markets.

When the euro was formed back in 1992, there were several critics who argued that it was folly. They asked, how could you combine a large group of nations with very different economic landscapes and financial sensibilities under one umbrella, one currency, and one central bank? For example, as the strongest player, should Germany's central bank be governed the same way as a weak player like Greece? Now it seemed that the worst fears were coming to pass. With Greece's sinking fortunes tied to Europe's financial stability, the stronger nations were facing popular unrest. I saw that people in Germany were angry the way many Americans were angry in the face of bailouts a year earlier. They were asking, "Why should Germans, who have practiced fiscal responsibility, have to bail out the people of Greece for their bad spending habits?" The situation was reminiscent of the weekend on Wall Street when Hank Paulson and Tim Geithner tried to persuade big firms like Goldman Sachs, Citigroup, Morgan Stanley, JPMorgan, and others to create a fund to help Lehman or face the risk of going down themselves. A year and a half later, European leaders were trying to convince Germany, Italy, Ireland, and, to a lesser degree, Portugal and Spain to do the same for Greece. When the European Union and the International Monetary Fund came up with a bailout of $1 trillion, it was stunning. This was an extraordinary amount of money, and yet in the days following the announcement, the global markets plummeted. Investors were not convinced it would work.

It wasn't only European fortunes that were tied to Greece's crisis. There were implications for America as well. According to Moody's, Greece's debt was an untenable 115 percent of the country's economic output. No one I talked to saw U.S. debt escalating to levels as high as Greece's, but one investor I spoke with off the record—a leading investor in China—shared with me important information about one possible consequence that could have a major impact on the economy here. This investor was very concerned about U.S. debt because he said that 50 percent of China's wealth was invested in our debt. If our situation did not improve, he told me that China would scale back its buying of debt. The outcome: we'd probably have to raise interest rates to make the debt more attractive to investors, and that would likely have ripple effects on interest rates domestically, affecting everything from bonds to the housing market.

Again, it was a sobering picture of the consequences of too

much debt. As we watched riots break out in Athens over the prospect of skyrocketing taxes and the brutal sacrifices being imposed on a nation on the brink of failure, I couldn't help thinking that we should be taking a lesson from the crisis abroad. Imagine a scenario where the U.S. government would announce simultaneously a huge tax hike, a wage freeze, a spike in the price of oil, delayed retirement, higher interest rates, higher unemployment, and a generally depressed standard of living across the board. While such a scenario was not likely, it was not the stuff of science fiction, either. The sovereign debt crisis could place the American dream at risk.

In May 2010 I spoke to former president Clinton, and he cautioned against the mentality that we could spend our way into prosperity. "The American people have to take responsibility," he said. "You just can't keep saying you want more government than you want to pay for. And borrowing money from overseas, it's just not right. It's bad for our kids and grandkids, and it puts us in a very vulnerable position going forward. I simply don't think we can afford to keep exploding this debt."

It was questionable if even in the midst of failure Greece was getting the message. When I interviewed Greek finance minister Giorgos Papaconstantinou at the peak of the crisis, he seemed to want to blame not Greece's notorious overspending but the nature of investment activity. He criticized the lack of transparency in the financial system, particularly around collateralized debt obligations (CDOs), derivatives, and other instruments that "basically corner countries" that are trying to do the right thing and get their financial houses in order. That was one way of looking at it, but most experts were clear that Greece's problems were of its own making, and the solutions were going to cause a great deal of pain to the population. One observer compared Greece to a subprime homeowner who owed more than he could afford but who might find the cost of a rescue—rising taxes and spending cuts—intolerable.

I spoke with Nassim Taleb, a former Wall Street trader and author of *The Black Swan*, a critical view of the deception inherent in financial solutions. He emphasized that there was "massive fragility" in the markets that would not be alleviated by an infusion of cash. Granted, he told me, the rescue package for Greece by the European Central Bank and the International Monetary Fund briefly made things better. But, he said, "It's like putting a lot of Novocain on a decaying jaw. The infection is still spreading. You've got to do surgery, and people are afraid of surgery."

One person who was relatively sanguine about the perceived crisis was the former Bear Stearns chairman Ace Greenberg. He'd seen nearly six decades worth of market fluctuations. He was there when the Dow fell 45 percent in 1973. He was there on Black Monday in October 1987, and he famously said after a huge market drop, "Markets fluctuate. Next question." So when I asked him in June 2010 about concerns with the stability of the euro, he brushed them off. "I'm sorry Greece is having a problem," he said. "But Greece is a tiny country, even by the standards of Europe. And, you know, sometimes, Maria, markets go up and down for no reason. In 1987 the market went down 32 percent in two days, and that was the blue chips. The other stocks you couldn't even sell, so you didn't know how far down they went. They couldn't find a reason for why it went down. There was no reason. There were no changes. Over a short spell we made it all back; and it was just a question of, like in the West, enough thunder starts a stampede and everybody runs for the exit."

Greenberg's point wasn't exactly confidence inspiring. Nor did I believe that market activity was entirely random. The stock market was responding to real concerns on a global level. Greece might have been tiny, but it was the canary in the coal mine.

Professor Axel Weber, a European Central Bank Governing Counsel member and Germany's Bundesbank president, was among the small group putting together the bailout for Greece. He told me that Greece's problems were not a result of the global financial crisis, but its own failure to control spending over the years. "One thing that is clear is Greece had a fiscal deficit even in the good times of 2004, 2005, 2006," he said. "So the situation was that fiscal space was stretched at the starting condition, before this crisis. Greece is a special problem, and the Union is dealing with this problem going forward."

Weber's caution going forward demonstrated parallels with the efforts of our own Treasury Department to stabilize the economy and protect banks by footing the huge bill. But his primary message was one of fiscal responsibility. "It will be key to use the proceeds of this recovery that we're about to see in order to get to a sustainable starting position," he said. "That will be the lesson that has to be drawn. We need more fiscal responsibility in each and every member country. And the crisis told us that this is much more key to the Union than it has been perceived up till now." Weber's point was one that we needed to take to heart in America: Don't just relax into the recovery. Use it as a moment to get our house in order. Greece did nothing to pay down its debt during prosperous times. We are in danger of following the same path.

There was little question that Greece's main problem—spending money it did not have—was enabled by the same kind of financial maneuvering that nearly brought down Wall Street. When Papacon-stantinou was blaming investment banking activities for Greece's debt, he failed to mention that his country had welcomed the involvement on the part of Goldman Sachs that had allowed Greece to join the Union in the first place. According to a Bloomberg report, Goldman Sachs managed $15 billion of bond sales for Greece after arranging a currency swap that allowed the government to hide the extent of its deficit. These complicated swaps were perfectly legal, and Goldman earned a fat fee of around $300 million for arranging the deal. But like the broke homeowner living in a mansion, Greece was in over its head and didn't show it. And its grand facade was enabled by an investment banking system that was already breaking down.

Axel Weber turned a hard eye on the banking system as a whole. "Taxpayers around the world have put roughly twenty-five percent of global GDP on the table to deal with bank rescues," he pointed out. "They have a right to know whether this was a lack of risk management, whether it was simply some flaws in the system, where it was related to some unfortunate market developments, or whether deliberate attempts of fraud were on the line."

The drumbeat against the investment banking culture was growing louder, and Goldman was bearing much of the brunt, probably because the firm had been so successful for so long.

———

Lloyd Blankfein had long ago perfected an inscrutable demeanor. The Goldman Sachs chief was seldom in the news, and he rarely spoke to the media. He didn't really need to. Goldman was at the top of the pile, not scrambling for credibility or attention. It was a gold chip firm in a gold chip industry. Likewise, Blankfein was friendly but opaque when it came to sharing his views. Although he was known to be quick witted, he mostly kept his humor and his analysis to his inner circle.

In many respects, Goldman's reputation was impeccable; its success the envy of its peers. However, with the financial industry under the microscope, the media—egged on by a sometimes hysterical, conspiracy-theory-driven blogosphere—was intent on uncovering alleged special treatment afforded Goldman by the Feds. The implication was that there were old-boy ties between the 140-year-old firm and its alumni, many of whom went into government and public service. Some said that there was a revolving door between the halls of power at Goldman and the halls of power in Washington. An October 17, 2008, *New York Times* article, titled "The Guys From 'Government Sachs,'" created some discomfort in the ranks.

Even a partial alumni list of the firm was striking. Robert Rubin and Hank Paulson were both chairmen of Goldman before becoming secretary of the Treasury, as was Jon Corzine, prior to serving in the U.S. Senate and as governor of New Jersey. Stephen Friedman was a Goldman chief before becoming chairman of the New York Fed—a position he was forced to resign over purchase of Goldman stock. Bob Steel was at Goldman when he was recruited by Paulson to the Treasury. Paulson also called on other Goldman alumni at important moments during the financial crisis. He put Neel Kashkari, a thirty-five-year-old up-and-comer at the firm, in charge of managing TARP, and he pulled in Goldman director Ed Liddy to replace Bob Willumstad at AIG. Paulson himself had been recommended for the Treasury by White House chief of staff and Goldman alumnus Josh Bolten.

The Obama administration continued the trend. Goldman Sachs alumni include Bob Hormats, Hillary Clinton's economic adviser; Gary Gensler, head of the Commodities Futures Trading Commission; and Mark Patterson, Geithner's deputy in charge of overseeing TARP. In addition, the head of the NYSE, Duncan Niederauer, and the head of the New York Federal Reserve, William Dudley, both came from Goldman.

Finding Goldman alumni was like playing a game of Six Degrees of Separation. The links were amazing, although many critics questioned whether they were proper. Should so many alumni of Goldman be making decisions about whom to save and whom to bail out at the height of the financial crisis? Much of the grumbling about Goldman centered on the bailout of AIG. Goldman was a major counterparty of AIG's, and had the Feds not rushed to the rescue, Goldman would have taken a major hit. Instead, it would end up being paid 100 cents on the dollar for its AIG holdings.

The story of Goldman Sachs' connections went beyond who was in its family tree. There was also a question of family values. Granted, powerful companies often take extra heat from the eternal critics who contend that power always corrupts. But speak to certain Goldmanites and you hear a lot of chutzpah—including Blankfein's unfortunate comment to a reporter that he was just a banker "doing God's work." If so, God's pay scale was among the highest on earth. Hundreds of Goldman executives and traders received bonuses topping $1 million during the height of the crisis in 2008, and working there made Blankfein one of the richest men in the world.

He quipped to the *Times* of London in 2009, "I know I could slit my wrists and people would cheer."

Yet in many ways Blankfein represented the very best of the American dream. Raised in New York City, the son of a postal clerk, he was a lower-middle-class kid whose hard work and ambition landed him at Harvard and then at Harvard Law School. He joined Goldman Sachs in 1981, rising steadily up the ranks. When Paulson left the firm to become Treasury secretary, Blankfein stepped into the position of chairman and CEO.

Blankfein was a devoted husband and father of three, who shunned the limelight and the New York party circuit. He was poorly cast as a capitalist villain, and people close to him reported that he was stunned and angry when the SEC filed civil fraud charges against the firm on April 16, 2010, alleging that Goldman misled investors on a particular deal. The incident in question occurred some time before the height of the financial crisis, back in early 2007, when there were just beginning to be signs of stress. Goldman allowed John Paulson's firm—the hedge fund known for shorting the housing market—structure a deal called Abacus 2007-ACI, without notifying the primary investor that Paulson was involved in the selection. Would the buyer have invested in Abacus had it known the person on the other side of the trade actually selected the securities to bet against?

The last time Goldman Sachs made such a splash in the gossip columns was back in 1999, when Corzine, who had made Paulson his co-CEO, was dispatched in a bloodless coup spearheaded by Paulson and Chief Financial Officer John Thain. Paulson and Corzine had different styles and different visions for the white-shoe firm. In the decade to come, Goldman Sachs would reap phenomenal rewards and accumulate assets of more than $1 trillion. Now it was in the spotlight with an ugly word attached to its name—fraud. People may have envied Goldman, but truth be told, its reputation was solid, which helped it continue to thrive even during the financial crisis. The charges were coming against a firm that many people would say was the least likely to find itself in this position.

———

The news about Goldman Sachs came just as I was in the final stages of completing this book. Breaking news always vies with the longer-term analysis of a book project, but I felt the situation gave me a perfect opportunity to bring some deeper issues of the crisis to the forefront. More than any other firm, Goldman Sachs epitomized who we are as a capitalist society, and where we are headed. In the wake of the weekend that changed Wall Street, I found that Washington and the Street were connected as strongly as I'd ever seen them in my twenty years covering financial news, due in large measure to the cries for financial reform.

I felt that the timing of the SEC's announcement against Goldman was very curious. I couldn't recall a similar situation in which charges against a publicly traded company were announced during the trading day. In addition, the fact that the announcement came on the Friday before financial reform was going to be debated in Congress raised the question of whether politics, not alleged wrongdoing, was driving the charges. The SEC had missed a lot—

the worst financial crisis of the era, Bernie Madoff's Ponzi scheme, and more. Was this just a way to show that there was a new sheriff in town? Was it fair? Was it even provable?

Some people were grumbling that the SEC's suit smacked of political motivations. Later I asked SEC chairman Mary Schapiro if there was any basis to that suspicion. She denied it vigorously. "Let me just say point-blank that there was nothing political about this case. We bring hundreds of cases, every year. We've brought many cases coming out of the financial crisis, in fact. And we bring cases when we're ready to bring them, not based on really any predetermined calendar or predetermined perspective."

Still, I questioned the timing. And amazingly, when I Googled "Goldman fraud" one day, I came up with an ad for the Obama administration's financial regulation reform, asking for a political donation. Huh? Just as the SEC was coming out with the charges, there were e-mails being sent from President Obama to his constituents saying that America needed to get moving on financial reform. As I searched "Goldman Sachs SEC" on Google, two sponsored results popped up: one from Goldman titled "Goldman Sachs Website" and one from www.BarackObama.com titled "Help Change Wall Street."

One fact was undeniable: the charges represented a more aggressive SEC than we'd seen in a long time. That wasn't a bad thing. But when I spoke to a number of top-notch corporate attorneys, they were unanimous in the belief that it would be very difficult for the SEC to prove such a complicated case, involving sophisticated instruments and seasoned, high-stakes investors. There wasn't even unanimity within the SEC; the vote to bring the charges was 3 to 2.

Having said that, there was certainly an important issue of

corporate ethics underlying the charges. A few days after the announcement, I was speaking to an audience of around two hundred people in New Canaan, Connecticut. The audience wanted to know if there was anything new on the Goldman Sachs story. I said quite honestly that it was too soon to know whether fraud had actually occurred. One man asked me, "If you had only one question you could ask Lloyd Blankfein right now, what would it be?"

It was an excellent question. Looking out into the sea of faces, I could tell that these ordinary Americans, many of whom had suffered tremendous losses during the financial crisis, were in no mood to give Goldman the benefit of the doubt. I answered, "I'd ask if he thought what he allowed the firm to do was appropriate behavior toward his investment clients, and was it morally ethical." The room exploded in cheers, and that, I thought, was the heart of the matter. People wanted accountability. They felt that investment banks skirted ethics all the time, whenever it was lucrative to do so. They felt that these guys moving vast amounts of money just didn't care. It didn't matter whether it was true or not. Reputation is everything to an investment bank. It relies on trust, and if that trust is undermined, it can be brought down. So the SEC suit was deadly serious for Goldman Sachs.

It didn't help that one of the vice presidents named in the fraud charge, Fabrice Tourre, sent an embarrassing, self-congratulatory e-mail to a colleague: "Only potential survivor, the fabulous Fab . . . standing in the middle of all these complex, highly leveraged exotic trades . . ." In another e-mail, he described an investment vehicle that "has no purpose, which is absolutely conceptual and highly technical," thus confirming a public perception that high-stakes investing does nothing to support the fundamental health of the economy. Tourre became the poster boy for the arrogant, cutthroat culture of investment banking. It was not the image that Goldman Sachs needed at that moment.

———

On April 27, the Senate Permanent Subcommittee on Investigations, chaired by Senator Carl Levin, performed the familiar ritual of public accountability, calling a group of current and former Goldman Sachs executives, including Blankfein, to explain themselves. Such hearings are notorious opportunities for grandstanding, and those looking for illumination could hardly expect to receive any. True to form, the senators tried for eleven long hours to score points, using colorful metaphors, while the bankers ducked and weaved and labored to bury the issues in heavy layers of investment-speak.

In particular, Senator Claire McCaskell, reiterated a gambling metaphor: "You are the bookie; you are the house. You had less oversight than a pit boss in Las Vegas," she charged. The men at the table were hard-pressed to defend themselves and were mostly unresponsive. They clearly believed that the senators had little understanding of the complexities of their business, and in some respects that was true.

A source at Goldman Sachs, who was frustrated by the tone of the hearings, told me with a note of bitterness in his voice, "These hearings are never about clarity. The senators want to tar and feather our guys. They're looking for a scapegoat, and we're it. It's a public spectacle."

If anyone expected the tone to change once Blankfein took his seat late in the day, they were mistaken. During hours of questioning, he struggled to explain Goldman's position to the stony-faced senators, once acknowledging with frustration, "I'm trying to explain it and I wish I were better."

Reporting on the hearings throughout the day, I couldn't imagine how the average viewer—even one knowledgeable about investment banking—could draw any firm conclusions. At times it felt as if it were a large cleansing ritual, and what the senators were really saying was, "America almost crashed in 2008. Explain yourselves!" But while it would be impossible for anyone to determine, based on the hearings, whether Goldman was guilty of fraud, I did notice a striking stance, taken over and over, that may explain some of the dismay felt by American citizens. The executives became downright tongue-tied any time they were asked the simple question, "Do you have an obligation to represent the best interests of your clients?" The obvious answer, straight out of Client Services 101, is, "Yes, of course." But the Goldman executives seemed to have a hard time giving a straight answer. They were afraid to say the wrong thing after being lawyered up in preparation of the hearing.

In the end it didn't matter if the senators had scored any hits. In fact, I did not see any major body blows against Goldman during the hearings, and I believed fraud would be very hard to prove. However, the jury of public opinion voiced its upset. The gold-plated firm took a hit for sure. Goldman paid $550 million to settle with the SEC, putting an end to the potential tarnish of a legal fight.

TEN

Capitalism in the Balance

"The historical debate is over.
The answer is free-market capitalism."
—THOMAS FRIEDMAN

In the fall of 2009 I was invited to do an honorary teaching fellow-ship at Stanford University's Hoover Institution. It was exhilarating to be in the company of extremely bright MBA students who were preparing to enter the workforce. It was also quite a wake-up call.

I was taken aback when one after another of the students challenged me to defend capitalism. They asked, "Does this system really work? What's the value of the free market?" I could see in their eyes and in their words that they just didn't believe it anymore. My response sounded hollow, even to me, because although I had no doubt that capitalism is the most freedom-promoting and personally fulfilling economic system ever devised, I also knew that the financial collapse of 2008 and the bailouts of 2009 had failed so many people who believed in its basic tenet: hard work is rewarded.

The students were unwilling to blindly trust a system that had failed so miserably. Once again, the questions of "too big to fail" and why Americans had to rescue companies whose poor decisions had gotten them into trouble kept haunting the conversations I was having with students.

As I returned to New York City, I contemplated what the students had told me, in light of the events that had transpired since that crucial weekend in September 2008. Had we learned a valuable lesson and changed our ways, or were the changes merely the equivalent of shuffling deck chairs on the *Titanic*?

There is no question that easy money, too much liquidity, and way too much debt, along with greed and recklessness inside financial institutions and among individuals, had left the country damaged. For many decades the world had followed "the American way" and admired the United States. Now, after the crisis, that was changing. Under Secretary of State Bob Hormats told me, "For so long China looked to America for know-how. Now the Chinese have left the class." Europe and the Mideast—particularly in places like Dubai, whose fortunes had been undone by reckless and grandiose overbuilding—were contemplating how they would get out of the stranglehold of leverage and grow once again.

As the Stanford students suggested, capitalism itself had been damaged and was in the grip of a crisis of confidence. For the system to work, people have to trust that it will work for *them*. Instead, the public saw too many other people making a lot of money doing questionable deals, with countless lives turned upside down as a result. They saw the supposed guardians of the economy being careless with *their* money. For the first time in my memory, students were asking, "Is capitalism a force for good?"

The classic assumption that of course it is—an assumption under which I have operated throughout my life—had been upended. Embedded in the bedrock of the financial system is the presumption that the markets are always right, that they're self-correcting, and that the cream will ultimately rise to the top. Now people were questioning whether this is still true.

The students at Stanford challenged me, and others, to question the conscience of Wall Street. For them it was urgent. They were among the best and the brightest, trained and conditioned to enter a system that no longer seemed capable of supporting their dreams.

The Lehman weekend changed Wall Street, not because the failure of a single investment bank, or even the failure of several banks, was enough to implode an infrastructure that was centuries in the making. It changed Wall Street because it was a stunning moment when the confidence of a nation and the world was blown. Capitalism is not a tangible entity with inherent value, like a precious jewel. Its value is wholly dependent on public trust. When we say that capitalism is the best system in the world, that belief is based on the understanding that by and large the people involved will play fair.

Nor are investors merely abstract dealers or superrich fat cats. The most traumatic consequences of the financial crisis were felt by ordinary people, who lost their jobs, their homes, and their retirement savings through circumstances entirely beyond their control. They believed a basic tenet of capitalism, that everyone can get a shot at the brass ring, and the ring snapped in their fingers.

The famed free-market economist Milton Friedman spent his life arguing that capitalism was necessary for freedom. He fought against government intrusion in the markets, stating that it impeded that freedom—not to mention that it screwed things up. He once noted that if the federal government were put in charge of the Sahara Desert, within five years there would be a shortage of sand. Friedman died in 2006 at age ninety-three, during the height of the financial boom that preceded the fall. I wonder what he would say today about what occurred and what corrective measures should be taken. I am fairly certain that the advent of TARP and other government bailouts had Friedman spinning in his grave. And I doubt he'd agree to more stringent regulation.

The debate continues: what is the nature of capitalism, and what is the government's proper role?

One evening in early 2010, I had dinner with my friend Garry Kasparov. The world champion chess player has become a political activist and commentator. He told me he was writing a book about the financial system. Conversations with Kasparov are always thought-provoking, and this one was no different.

"Do you believe that Paulson did the right thing in pushing for TARP?" he asked me.

"I do," I replied. "It was a moment in time when government intervention was necessary."

He shook his head in disapproval. "Then you are not a free-market capitalist," he said. "Don't tell me you are. If you believe in bailouts, that flies in the face of free-market capitalism, which requires you to allow firms to fail. They made mistakes, they took on untenable risks, and they should have failed, so new companies could emerge."

Kasparov's position is one side of a vigorous discussion that is taking place across the country. But the systemic failure that necessitated TARP really was a remarkable situation—one that called for a flexible response. Emergency exceptions exist everywhere in our lives. We don't, for example, say that if a person can't earn money he should be allowed to starve. Our free-market principles make broad allowances for people in need. So, too, with a damaged system. Imagine what would have occurred in September 2008 if the federal government had said to all the banks and companies, "Sink or swim on your own." Perhaps the lights would have gone out on our economy.

Having said that, there is no question that TARP had problems in the way it was structured. I discussed this with Elizabeth Warren, the chair of the Congressional Oversight Panel, charged with reviewing TARP. Warren is well cast as the voice of oversight. A nononsense consumer advocate and professor at Harvard Law School, the fifty-year-old Warren speaks in the calm voice of a parent, but the impact of her words is knife sharp. When I asked her, "Where has the TARP money gone?" I was taken aback by her answer: "We not only do not know. We're never going to know."

I was briefly speechless. How could we not know?

Warren described how Paulson had failed to establish even minimal reporting procedures. "Secretary Paulson put this money into the largest institutions, and he didn't ask, 'How is this money going to be used?' He put it in and covered his eyes and said, 'I don't care how you spend it.' So we lost the ability to track it."

There will be arguments for a long time about whether TARP and the stimulus saved the economy. Alan Greenspan told me that it wasn't the stimulus that brought us back from the brink. It was a renewal of confidence in the stock market in early 2009. The markets bottomed on March 10 and rose for most of the year, making people feel richer and more optimistic. This, Greenspan said, was critical to the recovery, even if later in the year and into 2010, new worries emerged.

———

As the financial markets barreled into 2010, Congress was praying that the recovery would stick, while trying to respond to the anxiety people were feeling about their futures. The purpose of the financial-reform proposals that were making their way through the Senate and House was full of merit: protect consumers, rein in the speculative frenzy, stabilize the system, encourage legitimate growth, and prevent another financial crisis. But while most people agreed on the goals, the question of how to structure reform was more contentious.

In March I traveled to Washington and met with Barney Frank, the chairman of the House Financial Services Committee, about the elements he believed should be a part of financial reform. For Frank there were five essentials:

1. A systemic regulator to assure that no companies would be "too big to fail."

2. A resolution authority, giving the government the power to decide whom to pay and whom not to pay. Frank told me, "Hank Paulson said that his biggest problem when faced with Lehman Brothers was 'I either pay everyone or I pay no one. I paid no one because I didn't have the authority to shut parts down and save the rest. When AIG happened, I had to pay everyone.'"

3. A consumer financial protection agency to make certain that nothing fell through the cracks. Frank acknowledged that there were regulations on the books—credit card protections, etc.—but the banks managed to get around them, and this legislation would strengthen the protections.

4. Risk retention. "Thirty years ago," said Frank, "when you lent someone money, they paid you back and that was it. Today, you lend someone money, and then they sell the loan to someone else and someone else, spreading the risk. Under this legislation they would have to retain the risk for a period of time."

5. Transparency on derivatives, so we'd know where the derivatives were and who had exposure.

Frank was also interested in a proposal by former Federal Reserve chairman Volcker, dubbed the "Volcker Rule," that would allow regulators to restrict proprietary trading at specific banks if it was deemed to be a risk to the entire financial system or threaten the bank's safety. Volcker's position seemed logical: don't allow banks to use consumer deposit bases as their own checkbooks to trade. Separate so-called proprietary trading from deposit bases. It appeared simple enough, but precisely defining proprietary trading would pose yet another challenge. In Washington I spoke with several high-level sources who strongly believed that the Volcker Rule, as initially proposed, would never make it into law. For one thing, formulating a precise enough definition of what does and does not constitute proprietary trading "unrelated to serving their customers" would be difficult at best and probably impossible.

Notably, a discussion of the future of Fannie Mae and Freddie Mac was completely absent from financial-reform proposals, because, bluntly put, no one knew how to fix the mammoth mess. It was astounding, considering that the agencies held $5.3 trillion in mortgages. A frustrated insider complained to me, "How the government let Fannie and Freddie operate for the twenty-five years before 2008 was scandalous, and how the government now can fail to deal with them is even more scandalous." I couldn't find one person, on or off the record, who felt that a solution could be found while the economy was still fragile. "If the government were to stop supporting Fannie and Freddie as they are right now, that would cause a run on the government debt, as Fannie and Freddie debt is owned all over the world," said an analyst. In an interview with Senator Dodd he admitted that he would have liked to have seen Fannie and Freddie be a part of financial reform, but it just wasn't possible. "Nobody knows what to do with it," he told me candidly. "It's so big. Clearly you've got to replace Fannie and Freddie with some alternate idea. Frankly, no one knew exactly what they'd like to replace it with."

The issue is that Fannie Mae and Freddie Mac, being GSEs—government-sponsored entities—have the support of the U.S. Treasury but are also partly investor-owned and publicly traded like any other public company's stock. Companies, investors, and governments around the world buy their debt because of the belief that the U.S. Treasury will support them. As Frank told me in 2009, "We should not have entities that investors buy with a wink and a handshake that if anything goes awry, the U.S. Treasury will be there to bail them out." But so far there has been no change to that structure, although in mid-2010, the companies were forced to de-list from the New York Stock Exchange, and they moved to another exchange. They did this after failing to meet the minimum trading requirement of $1 a share for more than thirty days. Fannie Mae and Freddie Mac stock prices hit lows of 35 and 40 cents, down from 2007 highs in the mid-50s and mid-40s respectively. Their all-time highs were well above $100 a share. Meanwhile, the cost to taxpayers of government conservatorship continues to mount—$145.9 billion as of this writing, and expected to rise much higher.

While financial reform was moving forward in Washington, the situation on Wall Street remained volatile. One disturbing note was a consistently nervous market. Upswings did not involve broad investor participation. There were a variety of reasons. One, of course, was that the wounds of 2008 and the first part of 2009 had not yet healed. The money lost was so severe in many cases that people couldn't stomach the thought of losing even more. They opted for bonds and cash over the perceived risk of stocks. Banks were frozen, uncertain of the new expenses to come. A "flash crash" on May 6 didn't help matters. It was a scary day at the NYSE as we watched unprecedented activity.

The day started with a lot of nervousness over the situation in Greece. By the afternoon, huge sell orders were coming in without balancing buy orders. The NYSE operates under an auction system. If there is an overload of sellers, the specialist must be a buyer in order to make a market. Amid volatile activity, the NYSE decided to employ a temporary time-out, stopping trading on a handful of stocks that showed unusual trading levels so the specialists could analyze their next steps. These included widely held stocks like Procter & Gamble and Accenture. But during the ninety-second trading pause, the business didn't stop; it was diverted to other electronic traders. With no buyers, stocks plummeted, and the Dow dropped 1,000 points. It all happened in a flash.

The shocking event illuminated an uncomfortable reality: The NYSE may have stopped trading, but others didn't. There was no standard across all exchanges. It was like putting up a fence but leaving a giant hole in the middle. The SEC knew it but did nothing about it. In effect, the system was flawed, and we were lucky it didn't get much worse. Watching the Dow drop caused jitters, even though it recovered quickly.

SEC chairman Mary Schapiro told me it was a wake-up call, and the SEC acted very quickly. She summoned all the exchanges and said to them, "You're not leaving this room until we figure out not so much what went wrong, that'll take a little bit of time, but how do we deal with the symptoms and what happened?" She got a good response from the exchanges, and they set about establishing new controls that would prevent a recurrence. But the panic people felt on May 6 would take a while to subside.

This event brought me back to considering the question of confidence, the foundation of market strength. Did individual investors lack faith in the market? At the heart of investing is the idea that the stocks we buy will rise or fall based on the performance of an individual company, the state of a sector, or the health of the economy as a whole. If investors did not believe this to be the case—or, more pointedly, if they believed the game was rigged against them—they would stay away. Who could blame them?

———

By late spring, Barney Frank's committee in the House and Chris Dodd's committee in the Senate had each completed a financial-reform bill, and they were similar enough that legislators were confident they would be able to reconcile them in a legislative compromise acceptable to both parties. And they didn't waste any time making it happen.

On Friday, June 25, just as day was breaking, weary lawmakers emerged from a large conference room in the Dirksen Senate Office Building after twenty straight hours of negotiation. At the front of the crowd were Dodd and Frank, rumpled but smiling, with the announcement that financial reform was a reality. The newly named Dodd-Frank bill had passed committee and would move on for a vote in both chambers.

Frank, who had got some but not all of what he wanted, was ebullient in the media. "Uncertainty is the great enemy of markets, and we've now provided a framework of certainty," he boasted.

The primary elements of the bill were the following:

- The creation of a ten-member Financial Services Oversight Panel, composed of the Treasury secretary, the Federal Reserve chairman, a presidential appointee with insurance expertise, and heads of regulatory agencies and the new consumer protection bureau.

- The Consumer Financial Protection Agency would offer a number of protections on traditional financial products, such as checking accounts and credit cards.

- Greater oversight and transparency on the $615 trillion derivative market, stipulating that high-risk derivatives be traded on public exchanges and be insured by third-party clearinghouses.

- A modified version of the Volcker Rule, which would allow banks to invest up to 3 percent of their equity in proprietary trading.

- New oversight capability for the Federal Reserve, designed to prevent future collapses, particularly regarding financial entities dubbed "too big to fail," including an orderly liquidation process for ailing firms.

- New rules on executive pay that would require compensation to be set by independent directors and approved by shareholders.

Hefty taxes, totaling around $20 billion, for financial firms to pay for some of the bill's provisions. It was unclear how these taxes would be calculated, but this was one of the most controversial aspects of the bill.

The optimism of the dawn agreement began dissipating almost immediately. In the early hours of Monday, June 28, Senator Robert Byrd, ninety-two, died, robbing the Senate of a critical sixtieth vote on the bill. The timing of Byrd's passing was reminiscent of that of another Senate lion, Ted Kennedy, whose death earlier in the year made the passage of President Obama's health care bill uncertain. As a plan was under way for Byrd's body to lie in repose on the floor of the Senate, ironically, it was Kennedy's successor, Senator Scott Brown, one of a few Republicans who had been prepared to vote for the bill, who balked. Brown announced that he would no longer support the bill because of the $20 billion tax against large banks that was added in the final days of negotiation. Democrat Russ Feingold also said he would vote against the measure. Dodd's committee hurriedly regrouped to revisit the item, dropping the provision and salvaging Brown's support.

On July 15, the Senate passed the financial reform bill with a 60–39 vote tally. As President Obama prepared to sign it into law, the question was, what would the impact of the bill be? I spoke with many experts and began to piece together an idea of what impact it would have. Investors were initially encouraged that it was not as strict as many people had feared, particularly when it came to proprietary trading.

Some observers were skeptical about instituting yet another layer of bureaucracy with the Consumer Financial Protection Agency. Richard Bove, an analyst with Rochdale Securities, offered a reality check. "So now we're going to do a bunch of things," he said. "We're going to slap restrictions on the pricing in the credit card industry. We're going to slap restrictions on fees for insufficient funds or check bouncing. It's going to put the consumer in a much more difficult position, since the banks can't live with the rules the way they've been established." Bove predicted that as many as 14 million checking accounts, representing 10 million customers, might be closed—in effect, harming the very people the bill was supposed to help.

Another financial expert voiced concern with the limitations on derivatives trading, telling me, "This provision would require bank-holding companies to move their derivatives businesses out of their best capitalized, most regulated, and most creditworthy subsidiaries. This is the precise opposite of what the other derivatives provisions are intended to achieve—to reduce systemic risk by imposing capital requirements for derivatives dealers and major participants, increasing regulation, and reducing credit risk. The provision would put U.S. banks at a tremendous competitive disadvantage to foreign banks, which would be able to continue to operate their derivatives businesses out of their subsidiary banks outside of the United States" Indeed, a source of mine at Deutsche Bank had been practically giddy with the possibilities. "If the American government prevents derivative activity at banks, we're going to clean up," he said.

Banks were also trying to anticipate what effect the new capital requirements would have on them. The issue wasn't just the congressional package, but also new international rules, imposed as part of the Basel Accords, scheduled to take effect in 2012. The new rules would require much greater capital levels, which could have the effect of restricting lending. The thinking was, if a bank was worried about keeping capital high, it might be reluctant to lend.

I spoke with Vikram Pandit at the International Economic Forum in Russia in June 2010, and he told me, "I'm concerned about the Basel rules, not so much because of the impact they will have on us or most American banks. I think American banks are generally in very good shape, and we [Citigroup] certainly are as well. But the bigger impact is the amount of liquidity and the amount of capital they'd require you to hold is going to have a real impact on the amount of lending and credit creation in the world." Pandit cited a study that predicted a decline in GDP by almost 3 percent as a result of the requirements. "I mean, these are big numbers," he said. "We all want the banking system to be safe. There's nobody, by the way, who wants it more than I do, having been through what I've gone through, but we've got to make sure we don't make a false choice between bank safety on one hand and the underperforming economy on the other hand."

When I got back to New York, I ran into Pandit again, and he told me the Basel liquidity requirements for banks called for $3- to $5 trillion in liquidity. "Where do you think that three- to five trillion will come from?" he asked rhetorically. "The lending pool."

One of the biggest questions regarding financial reform was whether the new regulatory superagency would have the wherewithal to be more effective than the current agencies. A former chairman of the SEC told me that the agency didn't have the resources to properly regulate the industry. "How will the SEC manage the extensive new obligations it will have when regulatory reform passes?" he wondered. Under reform, the agency that missed Madoff and the financial crisis would have responsibility for ten thousand hedge funds previously unregulated, among other things.

When I spoke with Schapiro in June, I asked her point-blank if the SEC was capable of keeping up with the job. She acknowledged that there were only thirty-seven hundred people to handle thirty-five thousand regulated entities. "We do need more people," she agreed. "I think we're covering the waterfront right now—and we could do it more comprehensively, and that's our goal. And I will say Congress has been generous in the last two years to give us significant budget increases. But make no mistake about it, we are just now in 2010 getting back to the staffing levels that we enjoyed in 2005. And if you think about what's happened in our markets from 2005 to 2010, and to know this agency didn't grow at all during that period is pretty frightening." I had been hearing from others that the SEC couldn't keep up, due to staffing levels and pay levels and experience levels, and Schapiro seemed to agree that there was a steep hill to climb. But she suggested to me that the SEC has been able to tap into a new sense of patriotism that was bringing new blood into the public realm. She put a confident face on it, even knowing the huge challenges ahead.

In July 2010, I hosted an important panel discussion at the Aspen Ideas Festival. For more than ninety minutes before a packed auditorium, Alan Greenspan, David Rubenstein of the Carlyle Group, and the economist David Hale offered a clear and brutally honest analysis of where the economy was headed. There was agreement that a key priority was getting the business community spending again, but Greenspan and Rubenstein believed that the financial reform bill would probably accomplish just the opposite. Why? "The regulatory bill has an extraordinary amount of items that empower the regulators to implement and promulgate rules," Greenspan said. "I can tell you how it's going to play out, having been there." In effect, Greenspan said, the uncertainty created by a slew of unclear rules would discourage spending and lending. Rubenstein agreed. "The business community is in hibernation, sitting on cash. They don't know what the tax rates are going to be, what the regulation is going to be." He called upon the administration to end the demonization of the business community. "Often in Washington, they love employees but they hate employers," he observed.

Rubenstein, who I recalled felt so bullish back in 2007, was sober as he described a world where the economic momentum was shifting away from the United States. "We've been the biggest economy in the world since 1870," he said. "We will lose that title to China roughly around 2035." Ultimately, he suggested that the United States might be number three among world economies. "There's nothing the president or the Congress can do," he declared—not because they didn't have a role to play, but because the political will has been lacking when it comes to addressing real issues. "Congress is dysfunctional," he said, highlighting the overemphasis on vague regulations and the underemphasis on making hard choices. He concluded sadly, "Tough decisions don't get made in Congress." Indeed, many of the people I interviewed complained that the financial bill was a "political solution" whose value was more about the administration's scoring a win than about true reform.

In some respects, the public narrative was just as important as the regulatory environment—maybe even more so. Regulations fail; we've seen it time and again. The truth is, it's not possible to legislate perfection, even when the strictest regulations are in place. The health of the system is in the hands of the men and women who ply their trade in the halls of finance. I have spoken at length with hundreds of them—from top executives and heads of state to global investors and brokers and traders—and they all emphasize their willingness to rethink practices. Complicating their task is the rapidity of growth and change in a global marketplace where there are billions of players—long, short, buyers, and sellers. And that in itself is a form of checks and balances.

———

September is a cruel month for America. The attacks of September 11, 2001, took away the lives of thousands of people, many of whom worked on Wall Street. The events of September 12–14, 2008, destroyed the financial lives of countless others. In no way is a lost nest egg comparable to a lost life, and in no way can a comparison be drawn between the horrors of the terrorist flights and a financial setback, however painful and widespread. Still, there is one thing both events have in common: each in its own way was an assault on our way of life.

The financial debacle was a crisis of the capitalist system that is the underpinning of our economy and our national prosperity. Now, almost two years after the worst economic weekend the United States has seen since the Great Depression, we are still trying to figure out what went wrong and how to fix the system that failed.

Critics of Wall Street contend that the failure can be laid in the laps of the commercial bankers, investment bankers, and traders who took irresponsible risks and jeopardized not only the futures and savings of friends, family members, and fellow Americans but also the futures of young Americans who will be paying for the folly of the decade past for years to come.

Others maintain that the root of the problem were liberal policies that, especially through Fannie Mae and Freddie Mac, encouraged lending to tens of thousands of people who were not financially equipped to be homeowners. Still others blame the inattentive regulators, or the repeal of the Glass-Steagall Act. Clearly, there is no shortage of theories and blame to go around. But blame won't fix the system and restore the most crucial element of America's economic success: confidence.

In the best of all worlds, banks, investment firms, and major players such as AIG would be chastened by the devastation that their risk-taking wrought on America and would become stringent self-policemen of their own excesses. But let's not be naive that such a scenario is possible.

At the same time, one wonders if a raft of new regulations, such as those being proposed in Congress at this writing, is meaningful.

Many Republicans argue that larding on more rules by a bigfoot government is pointless since the regulations that were already in place either weren't implemented or didn't work. And, they point out, some of the rules being considered would put the U.S. financial industry at a disadvantage to foreign rivals. Some conservatives and Tea Party libertarians maintain that the whole problem would be solved if the dice rollers on Wall Street understood that there would never again be a bailout by Washington, and that no entity— corporate or financial—would ever be deemed too big to fail. All these debates continue as this book goes to press.

There will always be disagreements about the best way forward, but there are questions that are on everyone's mind: Have we learned our lesson? Are we going to be able to avoid another September 2008? My belief is that in the long run, no, we won't. And while that's sobering, it is also a function of capitalism as it is meant to be. Free markets are free markets. It's messy, but this very freedom is what we prize above all else. Companies are going to make mistakes again. Another time will come when there will be overleveraging. But that doesn't mean we shouldn't strive to do better, to allow the system to operate optimally and fulfill its highest purpose.

This is the bottom line: Capitalism—for all its flaws—is the system that protects our individual rights. The alternatives— communism, socialism, monarchy—have all proven less effective, and in some cases have led to a systemic breakdown manifested in poverty, terror, and the deaths of millions. Consider those societies that don't embrace capitalism—and freedom. So many of them do not advance. Even quasi-capitalist systems, such as those of China and Russia, have proved effective in raising up the downtrodden and chronically poor. On the other hand, North Korea and Cuba are examples of nations whose anticapitalist systems have led to decades of underdevelopment and misery. Capitalism, and the freedom it implies, has the power to give people hope and help them rise above restrictive regimes. For my part, I choose to be on the side of freedom.

Each afternoon, when I alight from my car on Broad Street in front of the New York Stock Exchange, I pause for a moment to look up. I have been doing this for sixteen years; it's an automatic response. There is majesty to the edifice, and its architectural grace is breathtaking. A massive American flag stretches across its portals, and above six sturdy Corinthian pillars is a marble sculpture by the artist John Quincy Adams Ward, titled *Integrity Protecting the Works of Man*. I have often reflected that the financial crisis happened because we entered a period when the system itself lacked integrity. The stratospheric rise of wealth, the high-risk leveraging, the absence of a stabilizing philosophy, brought even the mightiest firms to their knees. Now, as we struggle to recover, we must restore the fundamental principles. We must, once again, allow integrity to guide and protect us.

EPILOGUE

It has been almost three years since the weekend of September 15, 2008, but to me, it feels like it has been a lot longer. Three years after the worst beating the financial markets and global economy have sustained in decades, money is moving once again into all sorts of asset classes, liquidity is back in most markets, and things feel much better. On its face, it might feel as though Wall Street is back to business as usual. The Dow has made an amazing recovery since the dark days of September 2008. The big banks still have some problems, but there is no longer fear of massive failure. The AIG scare is over, and even the left-for-dead auto companies are experiencing some renewal. The ranks of big Wall Street firms have thinned, and there are far fewer hedge funds, but things have pretty much stabilized. Some people are still enjoying record paydays. In fact, it might be easy to forget how tough it felt when the market was down an amazing 50 percent from its 2008 highs to the lows reached on March 9, 2009.

So, America, has Wall Street really changed?

I believe the answer is yes. First, massive capital raises followed the government support and stimulus package, making the financial industry better capitalized and financially stronger. Capital levels are now solid at many banks and credit is improving. When the Treasury conducted its so-called stress tests in February of 2009, it raised the minimum Tier 1 common capital requirement from 2 percent to 4 percent, then raised it again to 5 percent and imposed a more stringent test. Banks now must demonstrate they can maintain a capital level of 5 percent throughout a highly stressed environment. The new international Basel 3 requirements may effectively raise that number to 10 percent for global banks. The government established a financial stability oversight council with the mandate of monitoring the financial system in its entirety. Vikram Pandit, CEO of Citigroup, called 2010 a turnaround year for the bank. It posted a profit once again and the government sold the rest of the more than 30 percent stake it acquired during the crisis. The government still owns the majority of AIG, but CEO Bob Benmosche has announced a plan to pay the money back, including a re-IPO in May of 2011. Many banks have begun raising dividends once again.

Liquidity and growth in markets outside of the United States have led to rapid global consolidation. Of course, in some cases, the consolidation was forced. After all, if someone had told me three years ago that in 2008 Lehman Brothers would declare bankruptcy, I would have thought that extraordinary enough. And yet to think about the number of failed or crippled firms that were either acquired, taken over by the government, bankrupt, or severely squeezed is extraordinary and a reminder of just how challenging this moment truly was. In no particular order: Bear Stearns, Lehman Brothers, Fannie Mae, Freddie Mac, AIG, Washington Mutual,

Merrill Lynch, Countrywide Financial, Citigroup, GM, Chrysler, GMAC, and Northern Rock, among many others. One of the things that made this crisis so deep was the fact that Lehman's failure came after the failure of Bear Stearns and Fannie Mae and Freddie Mac. And of course just days before the government takeover of AIG. It was the cumulative collapse of all of these institutions, many of which were overleveraged, that was so damaging.

These were among the most extraordinary and difficult years for the country and its financial system. As Jamie Dimon wrote in JPMorgan's annual letter to shareholders in 2010, "We have endured a once-in-a-generation economic, political, and social storm, the impact of which will continue to be felt for years or even decades to come." This moment in time was so dramatic, filmmakers have tried to bring the story to life in many movies. I have even played myself in three of them!

Three years later we are still feeling the impact of this epic period. More than 8 million jobs were lost in the 2008 recession. Today the unemployment rate remains at stubbornly high levels and wages have not moved much. The Federal Reserve was still at work stimulating the economy and financial markets in 2011. It grew its balance sheet to a record size, first during the crisis then after, as the central bank bought bonds as part of its $600 billion second quantitative easing program, dubbed QE2, with the goal of stimulating investments and economic activity. The Fed's balance sheet—a broad gauge of Fed lending to the financial system—expanded to $2.670 trillion in April 2011. The Fed's holding of U.S. government securities grew to $1.402 trillion. The Fed's bond-buying program helped confidence and the markets trade higher, even in the face of a slow economy, although many critics have complained so much easy money will lead to a new set of problems, including inflation.

The most persistent and toughest part of the recovery has been housing. Because of the mistakes in writing mortgages, the pipeline of foreclosures is steep. This part of the business remains weak throughout the economy. The banks will be fighting lawsuits for many years, from individuals, municipalities, and anyone else impacted by the bankruptcies and failed mortgages. Certainly one huge—and controversial—change is the regulatory environment. It has gotten tighter, and there is a parade of new enforcers on the scene, like Elizabeth Warren, who heads the new consumer protection agency. And at the Securities & Exchange Commission, chairman Mary Schapiro is putting more teeth into a regulator tarnished by scandals like the Bernie Madoff affair. The Dodd-Frank legislation created several additional regulators and set forth more than four hundred rules and regulations that need to be implemented by various regulatory bodies. Additional rules are coming from European regulators on liquidity and capital requirements emanating from Basel 3. Not that more rules and overseers are necessarily effective, as we have learned from the hundreds of overseers of AIG during the boom years. But even as Dodd-Frank is the freshly minted law of the land, many of the regulations are still being written and argued. We have not yet seen the effects of the new consumer protection agency nor has the "resolution authority," which essentially provides a bankruptcy process for big banks and is intended to isolate troubled institutions from impacting the rest of the economy, been tested. Many would say that today, we still face the myth of "too big to fail" after massive consolidations of financial giants. Among the consolidations: JPMorgan acquired Bear Stearns and Washington Mutual; Bank of America owns Merrill Lynch and Countrywide; Wells Fargo owns Wachovia; Morgan Stanley is a third owned by Asian companies; Morgan Stanley and Smith Barney combined their brokerage force; Citigroup has sold assets and is looking at emerging markets to grow.

The banks are still debating parts of Dodd-Frank, such as the Durbin Amendment capping debit card fees, derivatives legislation, and the international capital requirements. The resolution of some of these items will dictate how much consumers pay for general banking. Banks say the Durbin Amendment will cut $14 billion in revenue. Jamie Dimon told me once again in January 2011 that such reforms might actually end up being more expensive for customers as banks look for alternative ways to cover their expenses. "There is a cost of doing business," he said. "One of the ways you got paid was by charging on debit. . . . So banks will have to figure out other ways to charge for their product. I don't think the consumer is going to benefit at all from this change." He suggested that the Durbin Amendment could force minimum balances to go up, force cuts in reward programs, and maybe even limit the use of debit cards. There is also concern about the implications of derivatives legislation and its impact on market liquidity. Even as the economy stabilizes, the public remains skeptical of the investment community.

Many Americans still believe the game is rigged, and they want more acknowledgment from the banks that it was the hardworking taxpayers that came to their rescue. People are still upset by the bailouts. I have been surprised by how many people stop me—as happened at a recent dinner—to say things like, "Make sure you ask Vikram Pandit to thank us for bailing him out." At a recent conference, even a highly paid entertainment executive complained to me that Jamie Dimon had not shown enough humility over the mistakes his bank and others made during the boom times. Dimon was once the wonder boy of the crisis, and was still considered a winner in the upset, but he too finds himself at times on the hot seat, answering questions about JPMorgan Chase's connection to Bernie Madoff, and why the bank squeezed competitors during their toughest times in 2008.

Part of the negative public mood stems from the fact that three years after the financial disaster, there have been very few indictments, and even fewer convictions, over events that nearly sent the nation into another Great Depression. Added to that are some 8.4 million jobs lost in the recession, many of which have yet to come back. The Financial Crisis Inquiry Commission, headed by Philip Angelides, charged with investigating what went wrong in 2008, released its report in early 2011, and it was highly critical of both the banks and the government overseers. Ominously, Angelides told me this March that without government help, thirteen out of fourteen financial institutions would have gone broke. Angelides has been among those calling for further investigations and even criminal charges, but so far there have been no serious consequences for the people involved.

It does not help the public perception of Wall Street and business to see insider trading trials, such as Raj Rajaratnam's of Galleon Group, who was convicted of fraud in 2011, where prosecutors have pounded away at what they called a "network of greed and corruption." Likewise, confidence is tested when a lieutenant of one of the nation's most revered business leaders, Warren Buffett, is forced to resign for buying stock in a company Buffett's Berkshire Hathaway was to acquire weeks later. Scenarios like these have empowered a heavier hand of government as well. For example, using FBI wiretaps in the Galleon trial, similar to mob trials, prosecutors probed Rajaratnam's connections, which reached into some of the very highest echelons of corporate America and the financial community. These examples stoke the deeply held fears on Main Street that Wall Street can't be trusted. They also feed the political rhetoric that makes the Street a whipping post for all of America's troubles. For example, at Goldman, despite the best efforts of Lloyd Blankfein, the fear and loathing just won't stop. Even Jeff Immelt, the head of GE, who was appointed to President Obama's Jobs Council, has defended GE over its taxes in the wake of a *New York Times* article that questioned whether the company had skirted paying them in 2010. The familiar rhetoric of class warfare is still simmering and will undoubtedly come to a full boil before next year's presidential election.

Ken Lewis, who for a brief moment in the financial crisis looked like a hero when his Bank of America bought Merrill Lynch, is, of course, history. The new Bank of America chief executive, Brian Moynihan, is still struggling to fix a mortgage business crippled by foreclosures. The robo signings at Countrywide and other lenders continue to stifle earnings and economic growth. Moynihan told me in March 2011 that in spite of encouraging signs in the bank's other business, the housing crisis lingers. "Housing may go up or down, but it's had a big fall off, and now we have to work our way through it," he said. "We have a bubble of foreclosures and modifications that we've got to get through. We have consumers we've got to work with to restructure home ownership." In other words, there's a long slog ahead. The housing market has not participated in the economic recovery, and home prices are still falling. This in turn drags down other sectors of the economy and limits job growth.

But even with all of the questions, at the end of the day, America and its strong financial system survived. The last three years have been challenging and dramatic but also defining. Debt has taken on a greater negative connotation. Individuals are applying for less of it and paying down their credit more responsibly. People are also starting to save again. Nest eggs were up 9.2 percent in 2010, and total U.S. retirement assets rose to $17.5 trillion, the most since the end of 2007, when they totaled $17.9 trillion. The conversation over debt has shifted away from Wall Street and the individual to the government and its spending. As I write this, Congress is in the middle of an unprecedented discussion about raising the $14.3 trillion debt limit. This has become part of the national conversation, after a persistent debt crisis throughout Europe and austerity measures taking place throughout the world. People are asking, after what we experienced in 2008, can we keep borrowing more money than we take in?

Still, the economic story is much different, and much stronger today than it was three years ago, even as the debate continues over some of the decisions made during that fateful weekend. There are still those who believe the biggest mistake government made was not saving Lehman Brothers. In hindsight, these decisions all seem easy. But of course this moment in time was anything but. As former Federal Reserve chairman Alan Greenspan wrote in the spring of 2011, "The Lehman Brothers Bankruptcy in September of 2008 appears to have triggered the greatest global financial crisis ever . . . [when] global trade credit, commercial paper, and other key short term financial markets effectively closed." This is a cautionary tale about the fallibility of even the best and the brightest among us. This extraordinary period of economic crisis will be remembered for many decades to come. I hope that this book, and this new epilogue, can put the weekend that changed it all into context for you.

ACKNOWLEDGMENTS

I feel privileged that my work takes me daily inside the vital heart of the financial system and gives me an eyewitness perch from which to view events that will shape the nation for decades to come. Between personal interviews, interviews on my shows, *Closing Bell* and *Wall Street Journal Report,* and my column in *Business Week* I was able to be an eyewitness to this crisis. Because of such rare access, I have been able to write this account of the most significant financial upheaval in modern memory.

I could not have done it alone. I am grateful to the many people who helped make this book a reality. My collaborator, Catherine Whitney, provided invaluable assistance in helping me tell the story in the most powerful way. She helped shape and write this book and allowed the interviews with the players to come alive. My agent, Wayne Kabak, once again demonstrated his belief in me and supported this project from the start. Thanks, too, to Ciro Scotti, whose contribution to the concept and the text was important at every stage. From his help editing my column at *Business Week* magazine for five years, always trusting me about who we needed to hear from to his knowledge of this subject and editing this book, he helped carve and refine it. Adrian Zackheim at Portfolio / Penguin embraced this idea from the start and gave me the room to explore my ideas. Along with Adrian, Brooke Carey, and Natalie Horbachevsky helped to shepherd this project to its conclusion with great patience and resolve. The marketing and publicity teams were instrumental, especially Will Weisser and Amanda Pritzker.

I am particularly grateful to all the men and women inside the financial industry and government who shared their insights and recollections with me during the crisis and in its aftermath. They have been generous with their time in personal interviews as well as in their willingness to come on my shows, *Closing Bell* and *Wall Street Journal Report,* to help people understand events and what they mean. I would like to offer special thanks to Josef Ackerman, Amar Bhide, Richard Bove, Bill Clinton, Bob Diamond, Jamie Dimon, Mohamed El-Erian, Larry Fink, Barney Frank, Scott Friedheim, Tim Geithner, Ace Greenberg, Hank Greenberg, Alan Greenspan, Brad Hintz, Bob Hormats, Jeff Immelt, Garry Kasparov, Dick Kovacevich, Christine Lagarde, Ed Lazear, Ken Lewis, John Mack, Dan Mudd, Vikram Pandit, Paolo Pellegrini, Hank Paulson, Jim Rogers, Ken Rogoff, David Rubenstein, Mary Schapiro, Stephen Schwarzman, Robert Steel, John Thain, Paul Volcker, Axel Weber, Jack Welch, Jim Wilkinson, Meredith Whitney, and Robert Wolf. As always, I am thankful to those at the New York Stock Exchange who have allowed me such remarkable access.

I am deeply grateful to all the people at CNBC who make my work possible. Thanks to Mark Hoffman, who made it one of his priorities to increase the number of guests on CNBC every day. As anyone who is covering a story in real time knows, it is essential to speak to the insiders, and CNBC did just that during this crisis, and provided viewers with real perspective with extra live global coverage and the biggest names in business and government weighing in. CNBC helped put the crisis in context for millions. In particular, I could not do what I do without the daily commitment and creativity of the people on my team. Lulu Chiang makes it hapen every day with her amazing dedication and talent. She and Donna Burton have been instrumental in landing the kinds of guests everyone needs to hear from to best understand what is happening. The entire *Closing Bell* team, led by Alex Crippen and Han-Ting Wang, covered this story in real time. Thanks to Joel Franklin, Katie Kramer, and everyone on the *Wall Street Journal Report* for putting this unprecedented moment in time in real perspective. Thanks to Deborah Nikiper for providing unwavering daily support. I am lucky to have such a fantastic team, including everyone at cnbc.com who also covered this crisis on a daily basis.

The media is often criticized for different reasons, but I have to say how proud I am of all of my colleagues in the industry. Reporters everywhere—from CNBC to Bloomberg and Fox to the *Wall Street Journal*, the *New York Times, Financial Times,* the *Washington Post,* the wire and online news services, and many other business networks and publications—did remarkable work covering the worst financial crisis any of us had ever seen. Overall, the media did a great job handicapping complex issues and making them understandable and accessible for the public. Their coverage provided enormous value and critical information for investors, insiders, and consumers.

On a personal level, none of this would be possible without the ongoing support of my wonderful family, who remains the foundation of all that I do. Thanks so much, Jono, for always pushing me forward.

In the course of each year I interview hundreds of people for my two shows, *Closing Bell* and the *Wall Street Journal Report*. They represent a wide spectrum of positions and viewpoints—from corporation heads to Wall Street traders to industry leaders to academics to public officials and national and international government leaders and politicians. During the critical period surrounding the death of Lehman Brothers and the subsequent crisis in the financial industry, I called upon many of these sources to provide me with an inside view of events as they happened. Later I interviewed many others to gain insight on why the crisis occurred and how it changed Wall Street. When possible, I have put my sources on the record, although it is a fact of reporting that some people request anonymity, especially when they hold sensitive positions within government or corporations.

PROLOGUE: RIDING HIGH BEFORE THE FALL

8 Lunch at the Four Seasons with Stephen Schwarzman, January 23, 2006; interview notes.

9 Details of the sale of Equity Office Properties: Terry Priston, "Blackstone's Bid for Equity Office Prevails," *New York Times*, February 8, 2007.

9 I hosted *Charlie Rose* Monday, May 1, 2006; transcript at www.charlierose.com.

11 Descriptions of the two Schwarzman parties are from my personal recollections, but the events also received some media coverage, in particular: James B. Stewart, "The Birthday Party," *New Yorker*, February 11, 2008.

12 "It was a great age": Author interview with Mohamed El-Erian, March 15, 2010; transcript.

12 Schwarzman's birthday bash and his company's going public: On March 22,

2007, thirty days after Schwarzman's birthday party, Blackstone registered with the SEC to take the company public.

12 At the 2007 World Economic Forum in Davos, Switzerland, I interviewed a series of leaders regarding potential crises in the future and published their comments in my *BusinessWeek* column "Facetime with Maria Bartiromo," February 6, 2006. I later spoke with Josef Ackermann in Russia in June 2010, asking how he could have been so prescient.

14 "It's hard to believe": Author interview with David Rubenstein, January 15, 2007; transcript.

CHAPTER ONE: NIGHTMARE ON LIBERTY STREET

16 "The dominoes were falling": John Mack's remarks aired on my television special, *One Year Later: Reflections from the Street*, September 13, 2009, www.cnbc.com. I also interviewed Mack on several occasions before and after the crisis.

17 Paulson's calls to Lewis and his frame of mind about the rescue of Lehman Brothers were described to me in a taped interview with a Treasury official.

19 "By Friday . . . we just wanted to get through the damn day": Author interview with an executive close to Fuld; transcript.

20 The failed deal between Fuld and the Koreans was widely reported in the media and confirmed for me with sources inside Lehman Brothers.

21 "The world changed": Author interview with Mohamed El-Erian, September 12, 2008; transcript.

21 "They have their hat": Author interview with David Kelly, *Closing Bell*, September 12, 2008, www.cnbc.com.

21 "There is no reason": Author interview with Martin Feldstein, *Closing Bell*, September 12, 2008, www.cnbc.com.

21 "This is a sea change": Author interview with Jerry Webman, *Closing Bell*, September 12, 2008, www.cnbc.com.

24 "Everyone thought good ol' Hank would be there with the money": Told to me by a Treasury official; transcript.

25 Descriptions of what went on in the meetings at the Fed are from multiple sources, including interviews with Robert Wolf, John Mack, Vikram Pandit, Bob Diamond, Lehman executives, and Treasury officials; transcripts.

27 "There was a disconnect": Author interview with Larry McDonald, April 2008; transcript.

28 "To say Dick": Author interview with Lehman source, defending Fuld, on background.

29 Description of Bob Diamond's role and sentiments on September 12: Author interview with Bob Diamond, as well as remarks he made on my television special, *One Year Later: Reflections from the Street*; www.cnbc.com.

31 "The board is looking": Author interview with John Thain, after he became Merrill CEO, November 26, 2007; transcript.

33 "You had this sense": John Mack's recollections are in an interview for my television special, *One Year Later: Reflections from the Street*; www.cnbc.com.

33 Robert Wolf's recollections: Author interview February 18, 2010; transcript.

33 Vikram Pandit's recollections of being summoned to the Fed are in an interview for my television special, *One Year Later: Reflections from the Street*; www.cnbc.com.

34 One observer painted a remarkable picture for me: From a conversation with a Treasury official; transcript.

CHAPTER TWO: THE BUBBLE MACHINE

38 "It's not that events": Author interview with Ed Lazear, February 25, 2010; transcript.

39 "It's distressing": Author interview with Angelo Mozilo, March 26, 2007; transcript.

40 April 17, 2006, e-mail uncovered by federal investigators in 2009: Source: SEC complaint.

41 "We had a lot of people": Author interview with Angelo Mozilo, August 29, 2007; transcript.

42 "Every day I'd wake up": Author interview with Angelo Mozilo, December 2007; transcript.

42 Description of Ken Lewis's reasons for buying Countrywide: Author interview with Ken Lewis, January 16, 2008; transcript.

44 Alan Greenspan's "froth in the markets" comment was made in a speech to the Economic Club of New York, May 20, 2005.

44 Ben Bernanke's comments about the housing market: from his testimony at his confirmation hearing, November 15, 2005.

46 "We were only looking": Author interview with Paolo Pellegrini, February 12, 2010; transcript.

47 Accounts of Jimmy Cayne's behavior are from multiple sources, including Kate Kelly, "Bear CEO's Handling of Crisis Raises Issues," *Wall Street Journal*, November 1, 2007; my interview with former Bear Stearns chairman Alan Greenberg, June 11, 2010; and Alan "Ace" Greenberg, *The Rise and Fall of Bear Stearns* (New York: Simon & Schuster, 2010).

47 Ralph Cioffi and Everquest Financial details are from CNBC and other reporting as well as the indictment from the Eastern District of New York, June 19, 2008.

48 "His relationship with me": Author interview with Ace Greenberg, June 11, 2010. Portions aired on *Wall Street Journal Report*; transcript and www.cnbc.com.

50 "I don't get any joy out of anyone's pain": Author interview with Larry Fink, March 11, 2008; transcript.

50 Description of Alan Schwartz interview on CNBC defending Bear Stearns, March 12, 2008; www.cnbc.com.

53 "Jamie was incredibly smart": Author interview with Sandy Weill, October 22, 2006, partially published in my *BusinessWeek* column, "Facetime with Maria Bartiromo," titled "Sandy Weill's Wild Ride"; transcript.

54 "The news that Bear's": Timothy Geithner in testimony before the Senate Banking Committee, April 3, 2008; transcript.

56 "It's the last time": Author interview with Jamie Dimon, April 2008; transcript.

58 "My regret was": Author interview with Ace Greenberg, June 11, 2010; transcript.

58 "Well, you've had your big moment, Mr. Secretary": From author interview with a Treasury official.

CHAPTER THREE: ZOMBIES AT LEHMAN

59 "Across the table the Lehman guys truly looked like zombies": From a banking source inside the meetings; notes.

60 Description of phone calls between Paulson and Fuld: Author interview with Lehman executive on background; notes.

61 "When I heard people": Author interview with Scott Friedheim, February 10, 2010; transcript.

64 Callan in *Condé Nast Portfolio:* Sheelah Kolhatkar, "Wall Street's Most Powerful Woman," *Condé Nast Portfolio*, March 2008. Additional background on Callan is from an author interview, October 30, 2007, after she became Lehman CFO; transcript.

65 Author interview with Erin Callan, March 20, 2008; on *Closing Bell*, and partially published in my *BusinessWeek* column "Facetime with Maria Bartiromo"; www.cnbc.com; magazine and transcript.

65 "Good to see you": Author interview with Erin Callan, *Closing Bell*, April 1, 2008; www.cnbc.com.

66 Einhorn made the Lehman speech at the Ira W. Sohn Investment Research Conference, which coincided with the publication of his book, *Fooling Some of the People All of the Time* (Hoboken, NJ: John Wiley & Sons, 2008; www.greenlightcapital.com).

68 "If you're asking me": Author interview with Brad Hintz, June 4, 2008; transcript.

68 Paulson's calls to Fuld were described to me by a Treasury official close to the secretary; notes.

68 "It really became apparent over the summer that no one had the same view as Dick of what Lehman was worth": Background interview with a Treasury source; notes.

69 "Every weekend we were at the office, busted up into teams, discussing options": Description by Lehman executive on background; transcript.

69 Wednesday, June 4, 2008, *Wall Street Journal* article: Susanne Craig, "Lehman Is Seeking Overseas Capital: As Its Stock Declines, Wall Street Firm Expands Search For Cash, May Tap Korea."

70 Descriptions of the upset inside Lehman after the article was published are from interviews with former executives, including Friedheim; transcript.

71 "I've been crying": Author's personal conversation with Erin Callan.

72 "the marketplace": Larry Fink's recollections shared on my television special, *One Year Later: Recollections from the Street*; www.cnbc.com.

72 Optimistic sports analogies in mid-2008 are from Morgan Stanley CEO John Mack to shareholders: "The subprime crisis is in the eighth or ninth inning"; Goldman Sachs CEO Lloyd Blankfein: "We're probably in the third or fourth quarter of a four quarter game."

73 "**A lot of the managements**": Author interview with Brad Hintz, June 2008; transcript.

73 Description of Daniel Mudd's experience at Fannie Mae: Author interview with Daniel Mudd, March 8, 2010; transcript.

77 "**Some people thought Fannie was a bit stronger than Freddie**": From a conversation with a Treasury official; notes.

78 "**The problem was**": Author interview with Mohamed El-Erian, March 15, 2010; transcript.

79 "**Are there plans afoot**": Author interview with Hank Paulson on *Closing Bell*, September 10, 2008; transcript.

80 Details of the Friday evening call between Dick Fuld and Ken Lewis were recounted by a Lehman executive who was present.

———

CHAPTER FOUR: DOWN TO THE WIRE

83 "**We finished around midnight**": Early Saturday conversations with executive sources at Lehman Brothers; notes.

84 Saturday conversation with a trader at Lehman Brothers; notes.

85 Details of Paulson and Lewis's phone call were recounted by a Treasury official; transcript.

86 Details of Fuld's trying to get Lewis on the phone were recounted by an executive source at Lehman; notes.

87 Reports from the working groups were described by many sources inside the meetings, including Robert Wolf, Vikram Pandit, and John Mack; transcript.

88 "**I was pissed off because they were pounding us**": Recounted by a Treasury official; notes.

89 "**You have the thundering herd**": Recounted by a Treasury official; transcript.

92 Description of Hank Greenberg's role and sentiments: Multiple author interviews with Hank Greenberg; transcripts.

94 **He'd called Lehman "a great franchise"**: Author interview with Hank Greenberg, June 17, 2008; transcript.

96 "**Dick is amazing**": Conversation with a Lehman executive on background; notes.

96 "It looked like": Author interview with Robert Wolf, February 18, 2010; transcript.

_____

CHAPTER FIVE: DEATH SENTENCE AND CHAMPAGNE

99 Background on weekend events from September 14, 2008, are from the CNBC report "Lehman CEO sees star fade as firm faces bankruptcy"; www.cnbc.com.

100 Description of Bob Diamond's actions the morning of September 13: Author interview with Bob Diamond, September 17, 2008; transcript.

101 "They kind of strung us along": Recollection of a Paulson aide; notes.

104 "People have said, 'But why couldn't you have done something to facilitate a purchase?'": Conversation with a Treasury official; transcript.

105 "there was still a big elephant in the room": Author interview with Robert Wolf, February 18, 2010; transcript.

_____

CHAPTER SIX: FALLOUT

108 Win Smith's bitterness about O'Neal and the plight of Merrill: Author interviews plus Smith's document to a special December 2008 shareholders meeting, "A Proper Eulogy," which Smith made available to me.

110 Descriptions of Lewis-Thain press conference. Eyewitness impressions and tape; www.cnbc.com.

112 After the press conference I sat down to tape a one-on-one interview with Ken Lewis, September 15, 2008; transcript.

113 "What are your thoughts?": Author interview with Win Smith on _Closing Bell_, September 15, 2008; www.cnbc.com.

114 Description of author interview with Meredith Whitney of Oppenheimer on _Closing Bell_, September 15, 2008; www.cnbc.com.

115 "Our days had been starting": Author interview with Mohamed El-Erian, March 15, 2010; transcript.

119 "I'm trying to figure out": Author interview with Bob Diamond, September 17, 2008; transcript.

120 Description of David Boies's advocacy on behalf of Hank Greenberg: Author interview with David Boies on _Closing Bell_, September 17, 2008; www.cnbc.com.

121 Text of the letter from Hank Greenberg to Bob Willumstad, supplied to me by David Boies.

122 "I would ask for less": Author interview with Hank Greenberg, September 16, 2008; transcript.

123 "I feel energized": Author interview with Ed Liddy, September 17, 2008; transcript.

124 "Dick and I had this conversation": Recollections of a friend and former colleague of Fuld; notes.

124 Description of Fuld's testimony before the House Committee on Oversight and Government Reform, October 7, 2008.

CHAPTER SEVEN: POPCORN AND DOMINOES

127 Details of John Mack's efforts are described in an interview for my television special, *One Year Later: Recollections from the Street*; www.cnbc.com. Mack also described these events in a leadership lecture at the Wharton School in September 2009.

131 Meetings at the White House described by two sources in the meetings; notes.

132 "There was no average day": Interview with Ed Lazear, who shared his recollections of the weeks following the Lehman bankruptcy, February 25, 2010; transcript.

136 the "intent was to get at the root": Author interview with Keith Hennessey on *Closing Bell*, September 19, 2008; www.cnbc.com.

136 Hank Paulson's testimony before the House Committee on Financial Services, November 18, 2008.

137 "Unless the Treasury decides": Interview with Ken Rogoff, Charles Schumer, and Andrew Cuomo, September 18, 2008; www.cnbc.com.

137 "I have enormous confidence": Interview with Amar Bhidé, January 7, 2009; transcript.

139 "We still have heavy regulations": Author interview with Bill Clinton, September 21, 2008; partially published in my *BusinessWeek* column "Facetime with Maria Bartiromo"; transcript.

141 "Yes, I found a flaw": Alan Greenspan's testimony October 2008, before the House Committee on Oversight and Government Reform.

142 "We obviously knew": White House official on the auto industry; notes.

142 "Whatever the reasons": Treasury official on the auto industry; notes.

143 "These are people": Author interview with Barney Frank.

144 "I'd like to see them": Author interview with Jim Rogers on TARP, February 2009.

145 "Do you worry": Author interview with Andrew Cuomo, March 17, 2009; on *Closing Bell*, transcript.

146 "In the last twelve months": This story was told to me by a former executive of Lehman Brothers.

CHAPTER EIGHT: THE AFTERSHOCKS

148 "It was getting": Author interview with Robert Steel, February 24, 2010; transcript.

150 "We just didn't make": Author interview with Dick Kovacevich on *Closing Bell*, October 3, 2008; www.cnbc.com.

150 "I know it's a better deal": Warren Buffett on CNBC, October 3, 2008; www.cnbc.com.

151 "Where are we": Author interview with Hank Paulson, on *Closing Bell*, January 12, 2009; transcript.

154 "The losses began": Author interview with Ken Lewis, February 10, 2009; transcript.

156 "Merrill paid out": Author interview with John Thain, January 26, 2009; transcript.

158 "Clearly, the losses": Author interview with Ken Lewis, February 10, 2009; transcript.

159 "We believe": Author interview with Andrew Cuomo.

160 "I was in Charlotte": Author interview with Brian Moynihan, December 18, 2009; transcript.

161 "In six months": Paulson told me this privately during a commercial break in our January 12, 2009, interview.

162 "We discussed the promise": Author interview with Prince Alwaleed, April 3, 2006, as recorded in my *Business Week* column "Facetime with Maria Bartiromo."

163 "Frankly speaking": Author interview with Prince Alwaleed, November 24, 2008; transcript.

163 **"How much heat"**: Author interview with Vikram Pandit, December 12, 2007; transcript.

164 **"They all took"**: Author interview with Jim Rogers, February 2009; transcript.

164 **A year after the weekend that changed Wall Street**: a description of my television special, *One Year Later: Reflections from the Street*; www.cnbc.com.

165 **"It has been"**: Author interview with Mohamed El-Erian, March 15, 2010; transcript.

166 **"Dick Fuld should publicly"**: Author interview with Larry McDonald, April 2008; transcript.

167 Description of House Financial Services Committee Lehman Brothers autopsy: Fuld testimony, April 20, 2010.

168 Discussion of "Repo 105-type issues": Author interview with Mary Schapiro, March 29, 2010; transcript.

169 **"The key point"**: Author interview with Tim Geithner, March 29, 2010; transcript.

CHAPTER NINE: A GREEK TRAGEDY

172 Statistics about foreign ownership of U.S. debt: Council on Foreign Relations report, June 22, 2010.

172 **"Russian officials had [earlier] made"**: Henry Paulson, *On the Brink: Inside the Race to Stop the Collapse of the Financial System* (New York: Business Plus, 2010).

173 **"Government money"**: Ken Rogoff's statements are in my panel discussion at the World Economic Forum in Davos, titled "The Next Global Crisis," January 2010; tape.

176 **"The American people"**: Interview with Bill Clinton, May 2010; transcript.

176 **It was questionable if even in the midst of failure Greece was getting the message**: Interview with Giorgos Papaconstantinou, March 19, 2010 (transcript).

177 **"It's like putting"**: Interview with Nassim Taleb, *Wall Street Journal Report*, June 18, 2010.

177 **"I'm sorry Greece"**: Author interview with Ace Greenberg, June 11, 2010; portions aired on *Wall Street Journal Report with Maria Bartiromo*; transcript.

178 **"One thing that is clear"**: Interview with Axel Weber, April 28, 2010; transcript.

179 Bloomberg report on Goldman Sachs and Greece, February 17, 2010.

180 "The Guys from 'Government Sachs'": *New York Times*, October 17, 2008.

181 "doing God's work": John Arlidge, "I'm Doing God's Work. Meet Mr. Goldman Sachs," *Times* (London), November 8, 2009. Blankfein also made the comment "I know I could slit my wrists and people would cheer."

184 "Let me just say point-blank": Author interview with Mary Schapiro, June 14, 2010; transcript.

186 Description of Goldman Sachs testimony: April 16, 2010, the Senate Permanent Subcommittee on Investigations, chaired by Senator Carl Levin; media reports.

CHAPTER TEN: CAPITALISM IN THE BALANCE

190 "For so long": Author interview with Bob Hormats, June 18, 2010; transcript.

193 "Where has the TARP money gone?": Author interview with Elizabeth Warren, March 29, 2010; transcript.

193 Conversation about the merits of TARP and the stimulus: Informal author interview with Alan Greenspan, March 29, 2010; notes.

194 In March I traveled to Washington and met with Barney Frank: Author interview with Barney Frank, March 29, 2010; notes.

198 "You're not leaving this room": Author interview with Mary Schapiro, June 14, 2010; transcript.

201 "So now we're going": Author interview with Richard Bove, June 1, 2010; transcript.

201 "This provision": A financial industry lawyer speaking on background, in an interview June 3, 2010; transcript.

202 "I'm concerned about the Basel rules": Author interview with Vikram Pandit, June 18, 2010; transcript.

203 "How will the SEC manage": Author conversation with a former chairman of the SEC, unattributed; notes.

203 "We do need more people": Author interview with Mary Schapiro, June 14, 2010; transcript.

204 My panel at the Aspen Ideas Festival, July 9, 2010, was titled "Views on America's Economy: At Home and Abroad."

INDEX

Iraq, 137
Ira W. Sohn Investment Research
    Conference, 66
Ireland, 136, 175
Isaac, Bill, 201
Italy, 175

Japan, 129, 130
Jordan, Vernon, 11
JPMorgan, 26, 211, 212
JPMorgan Chase, 11, 15, 16, 21, 29, 53, 69,
    120, 129, 142, 214
  Bear Stearns acquired by, 24, 32, 55–58,
    63, 80, 87

Kashkari, Neel, 180–81
Kasparov, Garry, 192–93
Kelly, David, 21
Kelly, Robert, 16
Kennedy, Edward M., 200
Kolhatkar, Sheelah, 64
Korea Development Bank (KDB), 20, 69
Korologos, Ann McLaughlin, 75–76
Kovacevich, Dick, 149–50

LaBelle, Patti, 12
Lazear, Ed, 37–38, 127, 132–36
Lehman Brothers, 10, 13, 59, 166
  attempted rescue of, 16–18, 24, 26–30,
    32–34, 59–60, 68–69, 79–81, 83–90,
    92, 94, 96–97, 99–106, 134, 180
  bankruptcy of, 102, 103–6, 118–20, 128,
    168, 210, 211, 216
  bankruptcy as possibility for, 21, 24, 26,
    34, 59, 97
  CEO working groups and, 34
  consequences of fall of, 32, 34, 86–87,
    88–89
  crisis at, 19–22, 27–29, 59–73, 92
  doomed executives of, 145–46, 166
  failure of, 110–16, 118, 124–26, 127, 130,
    132, 134, 148, 150, 152, 161, 166–68,
    170, 191, 194
  financials of, 34
  liquidity lacking in, 30
  Long-Term Capital Management rescue
    and, 25–26, 69
  North American investment banking
    business of, 118–19
  overseas capital sought by, 70–71
  stock ownership at, 22
  stock price of, 19, 21, 70, 84
  toxic assets of, 17–18, 85, 87, 96–97, 100

lending, 202
leverage, 12
  economy based on, 21–22
  excessive, 12, 21, 46, 114, 190, 206
  on housing, 46
leveraging, in real estate, 13
Levin, Carl, 186
Lewis, Donna, 86
Lewis, Ken, 42–43, 85, 99, 215
  Lehman and, 17–18, 80–81, 83, 85–86,
    96, 106
  Merrill Lynch buyout and, 89–90, 103,
    110–12
  Merrill Lynch fallout and departure of,
    152–61
"liar loans," 36
Liddy, Ed, 123, 180
life insurance, 92
liquidity, 12, 54, 56, 63, 123, 141, 191, 202–3
liquidity factories, 12
Long-Term Capital Management, 25–26, 69
Lynch, Eddie, 107

McCain, John, 113, 135, 139
McCarthy, Callum, 100–101
McCaskell, Claire, 186
McDade, Bart, 119
McDonald, Larry, 27–28, 166
McDonough, William, 25
Mack, John, 16–17, 32–33, 127–31, 147,
    165
Madoff, Bernie, 168, 183–84, 212, 214
material adverse change (MAC), 154, 158
MBNA, 43
media:
  Everquest scheme outed by, 47
  Goldman as target of, 180
  Mozilo's blaming of, 39–40
  resentment toward, 166
  Thain criticized by, 154–55
Merrill, Charlie, 107–8
Merrill Lynch, 11, 16, 26, 31, 59, 80, 164,
    211
  Bank of America buyout of, 89–90, 96,
    100, 103, 105–6, 107, 110–14, 118,
    119–20, 128–29, 134, 152–61, 212,
    215
  concerns about being next to fall at, 32,
    86–87, 88–89, 90
  Mother Merrill and core values of,
    107–10
  toxic assets of, 153, 156
Merrill Lynch International, 108

An insider's account of the three days that brought the financial world to its knees

September 12–14, 2008, marked the weekend that changed Wall Street, and the world, forever. Top CNBC anchor Maria Bartiromo was there in the middle of it all, getting firsthand comments and insights from decision makers on all sides of the crisis. What she reported in real time to her millions of CNBC and NBC viewers captured the events and the rationale behind the decisions that narrowly averted a total financial system collapse and the economic chaos that would have surely followed.

Drawing on her unprecedented access to top Wall Street players, global business leaders, and senior government officials, from treasury secretary Hank Paulson on down, Bartiromo's fascinating and authoritative book tells the inside story of the issues, conflicts, and motivations behind the rapid-fire events. She profiles the decision makers, explains their decisions, and explores the lingering, often troubling, consequences of those decisions in clear, concise, and compelling language.

She also tackles the big questions: What was the root cause of the crisis? What were the warning signs? Could the crisis have been avoided? How does it continue to impact our lives today? How much has Wall Street really changed?

The Weekend That Changed Wall Street is a fascinating, eye-opening read by the most respected and knowledgeable business journalist of our time.

> "One of the fifty people who shaped the last decade . . . The CNBC anchor has made the transition to the inner circle of the global business elite."
> —*THE FINANCIAL TIMES*

> "She has interviewed just about everyone who's anyone in finance and politics, from presidents and Federal Reserve chairmen to Middle Eastern sheikhs. Today, there are few, if any, CEOs in America who do not return her calls and fewer still who turn down a chance to be interviewed by her."
> —*VANITY FAIR*

www.mariabartiromo.com

A Portfolio/Penguin Book
Business/Finance

U.S.	$15.00
CAN.	$17.50
U.K.	£9.99